# UNCOMMON SENSE

# UNCOMMON SENSE

## The S.T.A.R. Approach to Life

**Bill Abbate**

*Published by:*
Messy Miracles Books



Paperback ISBN: 978-0-9828486-7-8
eBook ISBN: 978-0-9828486-8-5

Cover and Interior Design: Creative Publishing Book Design

# Table of Contents

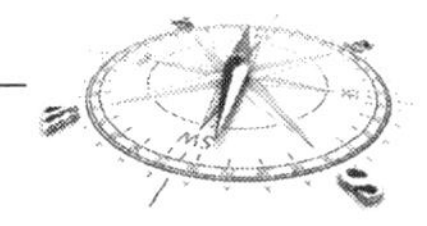

# Preface

Beep. Beep. Beep beep beep beep beep beep beep beep …

Waking up to that constant beeping sound after more than forty days in cardiac intensive care from four consecutive heart attacks—and then spending more than two additional weeks in pulmonary intensive care recovering from ARDS (acute respiratory distress syndrome)—I've come to an even deeper understanding of how truly precious time is.

When I finally woke up, breathing on a respirator, wires all over the place, several IVs, tubes in my throat and stomach (as well as other places I won't mention), I couldn't comprehend all that had happened. I certainly didn't think about work, money, the house, the cars, the boat, or anything else. All I wanted was to hold my wife's hand and enjoy every second of her presence. All that mattered to me was her and the important people in my life.

To say it was a *surprise* is an understatement. It shocked everyone, especially me, that someone who worked out regularly and watched his diet so carefully could almost die. The doctors and nurses at the hospital continue to refer to me as their "miracle patient," because it was a miracle I survived multiple *widow-maker* heart attacks, much less the ARDS. Most people are not so lucky.

I had written most of this book prior to developing health issues, and almost lost out on seeing it published. Much of what you will read in this book, along with a lot of prayer, helped me recover from literally learning how to walk and breathe again after nearly two months on my back.

Today, I am once again healthy and so thankful for my wife and the thousands of prayers prayed for me during that time and since. To say I am back, active, and full of life is an understatement! No one will ever convince me that prayer doesn't work!

While success and accomplishment are often mentioned throughout this work, I would be remiss if I did not point out my original and continued intent for the book. Yes, following these principles may well lead you to greater success and accomplishments in your life. Yet my purpose is much deeper than that. My heart's desire is to help you develop a more *significant* life, so when you leave this earth, you leave a legacy. In helping you and others, it helps me accomplish my goal to do the same.

For the past few decades, I have spent much time working on myself and helping others enhance their results, while also finding ways to lessen the stress so common in everyday life. It is my hope that this book will help you along that journey as well.

In this book, we will look at how you can become a person of significance, building an enduring legacy with the remaining time you have available. In doing so, your life will have lasting meaning as you continue to touch others well beyond your life. Isn't that a noble goal that would make your life worth living—to continue to touch people's lives and hearts after you're gone?

In all of this, I do not want to hide the fact that my worldview is that of a Christian. It is because of the hope I have in Christ and because of His many admonishments that we love and pour that love into others that I am driven to do the work I do. It is not for self-serving interests—it is other-serving that interests me, as a serving leader in this world.

At the end of my life, I want to have lived like a sequoia. When you see one of these magnificent trees, think about how it grows during its life—as tall as it can for as long as it can! It reaches to the heavens in worship of our Creator. My prayer for you is that you may live a life of significance, filled with Christ's love and purpose, creating a lasting legacy with your life.

In the end, may it be said: "Well done, thou good and faithful servant."

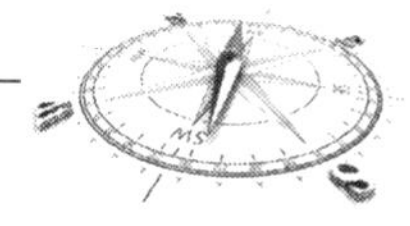

# Introduction

Your destiny is in your hands. Sure, we can hear that and nod in agreement, but do we truly believe it?

If you take a poll of successful people, the message will be resounding: It's up to *you* to build your own success. In other words, it's your choice to decide where you want to go. It's your responsibility to create a path to get there.

On one level, this statement is pure, simple, and true. Countless success stories support this premise. On the other hand, the statement can be infuriating. Most of us have multiple layers of blind spots, beliefs that do not serve us well, and obstacles that block our way to achieving the results we want. And of course, there is also the critical matter of how you define "success."

Throughout this book the acronym S.T.A.R. is used. What comes to mind when you look up at the stars at night? For millennia, stars have been used to guide those taking long journeys. It's estimated that light from the farthest stars has taken billions of years to reach the Earth. While there is debate about the actual age of the universe, the light from distant stars was created in the distant past. The closest star, our sun, provides immediate warmth, light, and life to the Earth. For us, what is represented in the S.T.A.R. acronym represents the opportunity to learn from the past and chart a course for a more fruitful life. While looking to the wisdom of the past for guidance, we can greatly change and influence our future path. We can move into the future with clarity and purpose.

While your path toward success may look more like random stepping stones toward an unknown destination, a few questions you must ask yourself can help you figure out how to reach the end goal.

What does success look like to you? How do you create a path that will get you where you want to go? And most importantly, how do you overcome the personal obstacles that hinder your ability to move forward with real results?

I struggled for years to answer these questions, and I have a mountain of journals to prove it. I read countless self-help books and listened to umpteen motivational speeches. Can I be completely honest with you? While much of this study inspired and fed me temporarily, it was more like an artificial sweetener rather than something that gave me lasting energy.

The information tasted great going down, but it left a bad aftertaste and I made minimal progress toward my goals. Little of it helped me make the real changes I needed to move forward.

With persistence, I eventually began to make changes and see results. It started with small insights and baby steps, but change began to happen. I could see the results I wanted so desperately in my life.

Over time, I noticed a pattern of positive change. Usually, change in my life started with asking deep questions. The answers, although sometimes disturbing, brought new insights and perspectives. The insights and expanded perspectives helped me see opportunities I had not noticed before.

As a result, I took actions that produced entirely different and new results. With each change, my life became more satisfying and more aligned with my own purpose, values, and goals.

I began learning this when I started asking myself this question: "What can I do to improve my performance, so that I can show I'm worth more than I'm currently being paid?"

At the time, we were struggling financially. I knew hard work and diligence would help me move ahead, yet I didn't want my job to overtake my life. As I continued to seek an easy answer to this question, I found how others had become successful, and I noticed that it hadn't been as easy as I had hoped.

I began to understand that I had a love for learning. I believed that, if I applied myself like so many others had, it would impact my career greatly. I worked hard, and over time, I read and learned from others, slowly advancing in my career.

This process became a lifelong pattern, which over time led me to one of the top positions in the largest company in my industry. And it all started because of acting on my love of learning!

Fast-forward to now. Positive change has impacted me so profoundly that I left a lucrative career in corporate America to retire early and become a professional coach. I chose to be a coach because I believe, through my personal and professional experience, that anyone can make changes toward the things that truly excite them, and that this will give them a more fulfilling life.

Now, I'm not talking about pie-in-the-sky stuff that may inspire us for a brief time and then dwindle into nothingness. Let's face it: Life brings many challenges and changes with it.

At this point in my life, I'm beginning to experience more and more that could be considered disheartening. I've seen friends and family die, watched careers seemingly end, and heard so much sad news. But I know there is another part of life—if only I open my eyes a little wider—in which I can make a difference. And I believe I can do so not only in my life, but in others' lives as well.

As I've worked through my own journey and coached others, I've uncovered a process that guides people through positive change. I am excited to share it with you in this book. I call it the S.T.A.R. Approach, because that's what it's all about: becoming the star in your life and shining your brightest.

While the S.T.A.R. Approach is simple and easy to understand, it will challenge you to "dig deep" and make some profound changes. Only through that work can you get the results you truly want, or dare I say, *need*.

The good news is that you can easily focus on one thing at a time and make one change at a time. Small changes will compound into significant results, and over time, those results will help you build the life of your dreams.

Here is how S.T.A.R. works:

**S** When you learn to **See** in new ways

**T** You begin to **Think** in new ways

**A** The door then opens for you to **Act** in new ways

**R** Which leads you to **Reap** new results

## The S.T.A.R. Approach Overview

We see in multiple ways, yet much of our *seeing* does not involve eyesight. If a person is literally blind—in the sense that he or she does not have eyesight—does it mean that person cannot see?

Quite the contrary, blind people still "see" in many ways, and quite clearly at that. The blind often have great *insight*. Meanwhile, those of us with working vision often see little more than what is right before our eyes.

We can develop multiple levels of sight and perspectives into situations that affect us and our behavior, the circumstances that surround us, and the results we reap.

So how is *your* inward sight? To find out if you have 20/20 vision in being able to see and understand your own motivations, behaviors, and self-inflicted limitations, ask yourself these questions:

- Am I able to listen and to develop new understanding?
- Can I consider other people's perspectives?
- Do I know the differences between my own needs and wants?
- Do I know the deepest sources of how I view myself and my abilities?

As in the analogy of eyesight, if your inner vision is less than 20/20, the "fix" is found in treating the vision impairment. Perhaps, like me, you need a prescription to correct your inner and outer vision.

This is the first and most important question on our journey. To see clearly within, we must first become aware of the need to correct our sight. We must understand what creates the results that we reap from what we think, do, and act on.

How do we do this? We do it by gaining additional perspectives; by learning and growing; through maturing; and by applying specific principles, some of which we will discuss in this book.

Remember, we also reap consequences from what we do *not* think about and do *not* choose to do. We can easily be led by things we neither see nor think about. How many times have you done something in your life thoughtlessly, and then regretted it? When we understand the things that we are doing blindly, we position ourselves to have different outcomes.

What is real and what is an illusion? There is far more beyond what our eyes show us and what our thoughts currently perceive. Typically, our perspectives are limited when it comes to the possibilities we think are available. Seeing in new ways allows us to see things we were not aware of and understand things we did not previously comprehend. This awareness is vital if you want to learn, commit, practice, change, and grow.

As you move through each day of your life, how many of your actions are intentional, and how many are done on "autopilot"? The patterns we fall into and repeat over and over can consume an important part of our life.

For example, take the habit of unwinding in front of the TV for hours at a time. What if you recognize this is a serious time-waster and you cut the time you spend doing it in half, so you can have more time to speak with your spouse, kids, or a friend? What if you spent that time doing something constructive that helps move you toward what you want in the future?

There are hundreds of patterns in your life of things you do without thought. Once you see the patterns and realize the potential of doing something else, it can change the course of your life.

Let's quickly look at each of the four parts of the S.T.A.R. Approach.

**See—To notice, observe, become aware of, view, watch, recognize, or witness.** Most of us have limited insight when it comes to ourselves. For example, your spouse may call you stubborn, when you've always considered yourself flexible!

Why is this? First, each of us has filters through which we see. You've heard of looking at the world through rose-colored glasses? There's much truth to that old idiom, especially when it comes to our view of ourselves. We tend to see in the way we expect. In other words, we do not always see what is really there, but what we *think* is there. Our inner sight is often a distortion of reality—an illusion.

A positive, highly optimistic person might see through rose-colored glasses much of the time, not realizing that such a perspective is distorting reality. To the rose-colored glasses wearer, a con man might appear trustworthy and a scam might seem genuine.

At the opposite end of the spectrum, a person with an ingrained negative perspective may consistently see through "dark glasses." Those dark lenses, metaphorically speaking, filter out so much of the light that they make it difficult to see *anything* clearly. This person might view a great opportunity as a dangerous risk with a doom-and-gloom outcome.

We all know people on each end of the rose-colored to dark-shaded spectrum. You probably are somewhere in between, at least some of the time. How can you assess—realistically—where you are on this spectrum of bright and cheery to doom and gloom? Find out later in the book when we use this concept to examine ourselves.

**Think—To understand, reason, consider, comprehend, envision, make meaning.** Becoming aware leads to new ways of thinking. For our purposes, thinking is *making meaning*. When we think, we make meaning of what we see.

Sometimes, our thinking is straightforward. For example, you notice that you are dragging at three o'clock each day, so you might think about ways to overcome it. Or perhaps you realize a brief walk will help wake you up.

Sometimes things are more complicated. If you discovered your thinking is consistently negative at work, but optimistic at home, you should consider what is dragging you down at work. There may be any number of answers to that one. The important thing is that after you notice (see) something, you can *think* about what it means. That insight will help you decide the best way to *act* on it.

Our lives are full of patterns. When you set out to observe (see) these patterns, you can begin to examine (think) and understand them. Just the act of observing the many patterns in your life will help you understand what they mean. That, in turn, will position you to choose what you want to do with them.

When a pattern serves you well, you may want to keep or even enhance it. When a pattern does not serve you well, you may decide to modify or eliminate it. But without first seeing it—and then understanding what it means—the pattern will continue doing its thing, day in and day out, influencing your life in ways of which you are unaware.

As you notice and understand your patterns, pay attention to the emotions involved. Also pay attention to your thoughts, physical body reactions, and the effect on your entire being.

Keep asking: Why is this so? Real change involves the whole person, and patterns affect you on many levels, physically and mentally.

Your emotions provide valuable information that can help you better understand the cold, hard facts you observe. Our patterns reveal who we truly are: logical and emotional human beings.

Are you using your thinking ability as well as you can? Ask yourself two questions:

- What am I spending my time (life) thinking about?
- What could my future look like if I began thinking new thoughts?

Use your mind to uncover more of who you are and why you do what you do. Discard the things that do not serve you well; commit to building those that do serve you well; and add new things that will take you where you really want to go.

Let's go back to the example of spending time in front of the TV to unwind. (For some people, it's not watching TV but spending time online). How much of your life is invested in these activities? According to many sources the average American spends between four to five hours or more per day watching television and more than three hours per day online. Read that again—not *per week*, but *per day!*

What could you achieve if you took even a small part of this time and did something productive, like learning a new skill, studying up on your profession, or strengthening a relationship?

Have you heard of the 10,000-hour principle? It is said that to become world-class in any field requires investing 10,000 hours in it. That represents the average person's TV viewing and online time for about four years.

Now, few of us wish to become world-class in many things. But the 10,000-hour principle does raise the point that what you focus your time on, you become more proficient at doing. How much would you learn if you redirected even a small part of your unwinding time into something productive?

This is what happened to me when I began to understand that a little time each day learning about my industry could greatly aid my advancement. It did—with a tremendous result in the end.

Once you notice *(see)* something in a new way that can make an impact on your life, examine and consider *(think)* about what is causing it—and its potential to change and add to your life.

You can ask: When I look at what I see here, what do I think of it? Do I like what I'm seeing? Is it helping me receive the results I want?

Evaluate what you see in terms of its impact on your short-term and long-term desires, relationships, and sense of well-being. What meaning am I making of it all?

Should your answer be anything other than "I will let it be," you are ready for the next step. Define what you will commit to doing *(act)* to add, eradicate, or otherwise change what you have observed.

**Act—To do, move, step, accomplish, undertake, execute.** The answers to the previous questions will lead you either to accept things as they are or make you determined to *act* in new ways. For example, if you observe that you're unhappy at work, giving the situation an honest evaluation (thinking) will help reveal whether the problem is with you or the job. Sometimes the problem is the way you "see" the job, and a simple shift of perspective will make all the difference!

Thinking will lead you to discover the options you have to change the situation. Should you find a new company to work for? Pursue a new career? Find new ways to look for fulfilment in the job you have?

Deep evaluation, and considering your options, also will reveal whether or not you currently have the desire and courage to commit to change. If you're not ready to change, that's valuable information!

But let's say you've decided you are ready to change your work situation. You might conceivably decide to act in a whole range of ways, from speaking with a friend you trust, working with a coach or therapist, changing departments, getting more education, to applying for new jobs.

The action you take might involve baby steps or big steps, depending on what you see, what you think, and what action(s) you feel you are ready to commit to. You might even decide that, although you see that you're not satisfied and you know what you could do to change it, the timing is simply not right.

If you are near retirement age, you might simply accept the situation—for now.

Remember, no matter what you see or think, the choice about taking action is up to you. Inaction is also a choice, and sometimes more of the same is the right decision at the moment.

But if you decide this is the time to try something different, deliberate, thoughtful action that you commit to will lead to real change.

**Reap—To obtain, bring in, come to have, secure, realize, receive.** When you *see* things differently, begin to *think* differently, and then *act* differently, you will *reap* new results. When you reap gladly, you are likely to reap even more! You now have a chance to do something new, something different, something that will take you beyond where you are and beyond who you are now. You have a chance for growth.

You might have heard the adage, often attributed to Albert Einstein and Benjamin Franklin, amongst others: "The definition of insanity is doing the same thing over and over and expecting a different result."

How sane is *your* life in this context? What are you expecting? If you are expecting something to change, what are you doing to make that happen? What course adjustments have you made?

I also like this quote, attributed to John Foster Dulles: "The measure of success is not whether you have a tough problem to deal with, but whether it is the same problem you had last year." Do you want to repeat the past, or change it?

It's not a matter of insanity, or even intelligence. No matter how intelligent you are, it's easy to get stuck. It's easy to keep repeating the same behaviors to solve the same problems or overcome the same obstacles. It's easy to be dissatisfied with entire areas of your life, because after a while, you don't even see what's around you. You don't think about how you got there, so you don't know what to do differently … and you continue to reap the same results.

It's important to reap both the good and the bad results of your actions. Learn from both kinds of outcomes, and let them influence future actions. Appreciate your mistakes for the valuable lessons they carry. And appreciate the good things to draw more good things into your life. As the saying goes, "What you appreciate, appreciates."

Choose what you truly want and know that, whatever happens, you can always plot a new course of action.

## What to Expect from This Book

I invite you to join me on a journey. Together, we'll ask deep questions, walk through some exercises, and explore examples that help us to see, think, and act differently.

Why do all this hard work? The fruit of your labor will be the realization of different, better results. By truly seeing, thinking, and acting, you can find the change you need in the deepest part of your being.

This journey is very personal. No one can tell you what kind of life you want to live. It won't always be a smooth path, because change only comes when you ask deep questions and answer them honestly. It requires taking time to think and reflect. No one else can do it for you.

When, in the course of your journey, you encounter a blind spot or unhealthy thinking, you must find the courage to act differently. Change isn't comfortable, but it's required if you want different results.

You have few basic choices in life: Either choose your own destination, or let your habits and reactions choose it for you—or worse, find yourself subject to someone else's ideas about your life.

I've been on this path for many years now. I've put in my own work, and I regularly partner with others in their journeys. And yes, I am *still* on my own journey. I'll be sharing some of it with you throughout these pages.

The result of what we will do together is not a solution to all your problems, but rather an ongoing creation of what we wish to achieve. It's one of those trips where no one ever arrives— rather, we continue growing and changing until life no longer exists in this current form.

Ready? I want to challenge you to take the first step. Take just one small step, this week. Don't try to change everything in your life at once, but rather take *one small step* in the direction you want to go. Just by doing that, you can change the trajectory of your life and create something good and something new. If you take that first small step, subsequent steps will become clearer.

If you don't know what that first step is, keep reading, and we will find it together.

This book is divided into three sections.

- **In Section 1**, we will go through each of the four parts of S.T.A.R. This will provide you with a quick and concise overview of the Approach.
- **In Section 2**, we will dig deeper to develop a greater ability to see in new ways, think new thoughts, act in new ways, and reap new results.
- **In Section 3**, you will find exercises and resources to help you integrate new ways of seeing, thinking, and acting, so you can reap what you really need in life.

Each part of this book is written in a way that allows you to use the book as a resource for later. You can always return to reading it if you get stuck. You'll find ways here to continue to deepen your learning as you change your life.

I recommend you work through the book slowly, giving each section your careful attention. It's not the reading that will move you forward, but the thoughtful refection on what you read that can help you make new choices.

My promise to you is this: If you read each section, and complete the exercises in this book, by the last page, you'll be a different person. Your life will be on a different course, and you'll be headed somewhere other than where you are now headed.

Let's get started by building the foundation that will help you become the STAR of your own story!

# SECTION 1

# Challenge Accepted!

# Overview

As we traverse the road of life, the journey teaches us many lessons. Our experiences and relationships shape us, influencing who we are. Realizing this simple truth can provide new opportunities to change and grow as we navigate through the ups and downs.

Each day we face a challenge: How will we respond to life's developments? How will we choose to act? This is where meaningful change begins. We must deepen our awareness and pay attention if we are to make change work *for* and *with* us, because our choices will affect the rate and direction of our growth.

Change is one of the only things you can be certain of in life. It's inevitable. But how you respond is up to you. You can allow changes in your life to control you, or you can take control and leverage change, creating something new, different, and better.

Who is in charge of *your* life? Are you following someone else's lead, or are you leading yourself? When your choices guide the outcome, you essentially *take the lead*. That's why it's important to develop your leadership skills. No matter what kind of job you have, your number one job will always be leading yourself.

So, how do you nurture your self-leadership skills? How do you guide yourself toward positive growth?

Like every big endeavor, it's a step-by-step process. The first step is discovering what you need. What are your goals for this? What kind of qualities do you want to possess?

In the following pages, we will be talking about change. We'll also explore ways in which you can use change to create outcomes that are in line with what you truly need in life. You can learn to use change in ways that better serve you.

Believe it or not, you're already on a path—but it might not be a path of your conscious choosing. What you have or have not done already has set your life on a definite trajectory into the future. But you can change direction at any moment. By making small course corrections now, you can produce better outcomes, winding up at an entirely different place in life.

If you want your life to produce something new, you need to see new things, think new thoughts, and act in new ways to create and reap completely new results.

Can you see how our S.T.A.R. Approach applies to change? Without seeing, we are blind. But when we can see something, we can think in a new way about it. As we think about it, we can modify our behavior and act in a new way as well. This new action will inevitably produce a new result. And because this process continues throughout life, new results enhance our ability to see in new ways.

If it's so easy, why do so many people feel they are lost? Why do so many lives seem "out of control"? That's because sometimes, managing change is more than a one-person job! You probably need information that's not already in your head.

Not one of us has all of the right answers needed to actively shape the outcome of our lives. But when two people come together—as you and I will in this book—we can make better things happen.

Achieving better results in life doesn't have to be complex. The foundation for growth is learning to ask better questions, which will result in far better answers and more options than you now have.

When your own thoughtful questions lead to more powerful answers, you can take charge in a greater way. Your own actions can help you grow and flourish in ways you've never thought possible. With the right tools, you can look beyond the normal questions and answers, which will give you a glimpse into a world of endless opportunities.

When I started a career in sales, many years ago, I began asking: What can I do to improve my results? What do the best salesmen actually do to become the best? How do they act? What do they study? Those questions were the basis of a new journey for me.

My curiosity led me into a lifelong adventure of learning. I started small, listening to recordings by successful people as I drove from one sales appointment to another. What I learned literally propelled my career and changed my life in ways I could not have imagined when I was younger. To this day, I continue to benefit from the simple lessons I learned back then, driving my old Buick Century down the highways of the East Coast.

The goal of this section is not to give you all the answers, but to give you a place to start. I challenge you to think in a new way about what you want—in your work, your family, and every area of your life. Then we'll explore new ways of seeing, thinking, and acting about your needs.

We'll help you generate the potential for enormous opportunities to take you far beyond where you are currently headed, and into a more fulfilling future.

Take a few minutes to consider these questions:

- Who am I now, and who am I becoming?
- Who do I want to be?
- How do I want to spend the rest of my life?
- How do I want to be remembered at the end of my life?

When you discover how to clearly see who you are, and then realize who you are becoming, you have a catalyst for change.

Let's take an example:

Who am I now?

> "I'm a hard worker. I focus on my job more than anything else, certainly more than entertainment or my family or home life."

Who am I becoming?

> "I'm becoming an expert in my field. I'm getting older. I'm saving for retirement, but by the time I get there, my family will have changed. My kids will be grown up and gone. If I look at it honestly, I'm eventually going to become an old man who barely knows his family."

For this person, honestly considering his future revealed a problem. He was neglecting his family so he could be more successful. His answers led him to other important questions:

> "Is this how I want my life to be? Am I willing to lose my family for the sake of my job?"

These questions gave him the chance to make changes that might redirect his life.

To come to this self-realization, you need to begin to consider the possibilities of who you truly want to become. Is your current life helping you become that person?

We can always change. You can become more aware of others' needs. You can enjoy life more, pursue better health, or accomplish whatever goal is important to you—if you take a greater role in shaping your ideal future. If you awaken to who you can become, you might not be satisfied with trudging down the same old path ... which will lead you to where?

Do you accept the challenge to embrace a better, happier version of yourself? Let's get started!

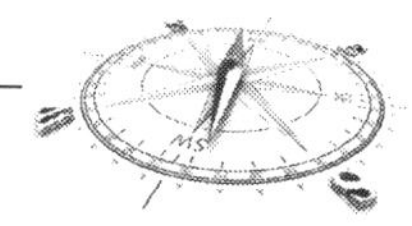

CHAPTER 1

# — SEE — The Gift of Sight

*"I see my path, but I don't know where it leads.*
*Not knowing where I'm going is what inspires me to travel it."*
—Rosalia de Castro

One day a husband asked his wife, "Honey, do you think I need glasses?" To which she replied, "I'm not sure, but you're trying to make a phone call with the TV remote!"

How is your vision? Is it 20/20? If not, you can correct it with the right eyeglass prescription. You can also get surgery to correct your vision permanently. But eyesight is not what this chapter is about. Rather, let's take a look at other ways in which we *see*.

The kind of vision we need to develop can be called "insight," and it has nothing to do with lenses or refraction. One definition from the *Oxford Dictionary* of *seeing* is to "discern or deduce mentally after reflection or from information; to come to know."

This kind of seeing is vital if you want to change and grow. If you're just seeing with your eyes and not your brain, life might try to point that out to you with experiences that "open your eyes."

When I started in business as a young man, I had very limited knowledge about what it took to run a business. I started at a relatively low position, where I was exposed to part of the manufacturing process. My whole world revolved around manufacturing for a time. I really got to know the ins and outs of manufacturing—but I was unaware of many other aspects of the total business.

As I accepted other positions within that company, I was trained in other parts of the business. My work expanded until I could see more of what it took to make a business run. Yet even then, what I could see was relatively limited.

Eventually, I was promoted to manager and found there was another whole world to which I had never been exposed—a world that included operations, administration, finances, marketing, sales, and so much more! Sure, I had seen bits and pieces of these functions in all my previous positions—but until I was responsible for making things work, I had no real understanding of how all these facets worked together.

From my "view" at the top, I could see far more than I could have imagined. I began to understand what was involved in making a payroll—and yet, by this point, I knew how much I still *didn't* know. I had a great deal more to learn before I could run a business, and even start larger companies of my own.

You probably have areas of your life where you learned and gained greater insight as your experience deepened. These most likely include changes you underwent in school, in work, and in relationships. You might already know that if something seems simple in the beginning, it's because you don't have a complete grasp of what will be involved. You're only seeing a small part of the picture.

Here are some other challenging questions you can ask yourself:

- How is my inward sight?
- Do I have 20/20 vision when it comes to seeing and understanding the circumstances and situations in my life?
- Do I "see" where the results I reap come from?

If you feel clueless about evaluating yourself, look into some of the circumstances in your life. For example, when your wife becomes angry, do you know what caused it? Is her emotional state a reaction to something you've done? If you have good insight here, it can guide you to repairing a broken relationship.

Or let's say you are middle-aged and you can't stop thinking about how much you hate your job. Maybe you're considering a major career change. Do you understand all the factors that led you to this moment? Are you reacting to circumstances in your work, or is there a deeper need to change professions to something that's a better match for your skills and values? How much time have you spent reflecting, studying, and talking with your family, people in that field, and others to develop the insight needed to make a sound decision?

When you make every decision based on how you feel on the surface, without looking very deeply, you run the risk of mistaking emotion for a true understanding of reality. You might be only seeing a reflection of the surface of the situation—or even a mirage, something unreal that only appears to be there!

There's far more to most situations than what our eyes and our initial thoughts show us. We have to allow that there might be factors beyond our current awareness.

Most of us are locked into a given place or perspective. Yet what other ways of seeing are there? What exists in the unseen, unknown, or not yet understood?

When I was working at that job I mentioned, I began without even knowing what I didn't know. As I rose through the ranks, I came to a much deeper understanding of the complexity of that business. At first, I could not see what I didn't know existed. But over time, that changed, and I developed an awareness I just couldn't grasp early on.

Our perspectives are often limited, compared to the possibilities that exist. To be able to see in new ways allows us to realize things we're not currently aware of and understand things we did not comprehend. In this section of the book, we will talk about ways to enhance our sight, remove blinders, gain new perspectives, and broaden and deepen our awareness.

You might be wondering: Where does our external and internal vision come from? The truth is, it comes from who we are on the inside, from the very essence of our being. That's because, who we are at our core determines everything we see, how we see it, and even how our vision will change over time.

## Seeing Is Believing ... or Is It?

How do you see the world? Does it look like a friendly place? Does it feel that the world is *on your side*, for the most part? Or do you see the world as a place that works against you, causing you to always be on guard? Perhaps you see it in some other light. Ask yourself: How *do* I see the world?

An even more important question is: How do I see myself? Most of us have limited insight when it comes to ourselves. Why is this?

First, each of us makes numerous assumptions, which create thought filters. As we mentioned before, "rose-colored glasses" refers to an optimistic worldview filtered by one's experiences. There's much truth to that old idiom. We do tend to see in the way we want to see or have been conditioned to see—and in most cases, if our view if skewed, we are completely unaware of that fact.

How do you know where you are on the spectrum of bright and cheery to doom and gloom? Let's take a simple test. Think about where your frame of mind is at this very moment. Rate it on the following scale:

Very negative 0 —— 5 Neutral —— 10 Very positive

For me, at this moment, I'm at a rather neutral point of **5**. Not very positive or negative. Where are you?

Now think about a recent experience that was emotional. It could be anything. For me, I am thinking about a conversation I just had where the person was complaining a lot. I went immediately down to a **2** or so on the above scale, and remained at that level for quite a while afterwards. Then I spoke with my wife about the weekend and moved to a very positive **8**. And so it goes with what I am seeing throughout the day, up and down, back and forth. Such is life.

*What just happened? And why is this important?*

The first important facet of "seeing" in a new way is to simply pay attention to something you had not observed before or haven't normally paid attention to. This is the simple act of *noticing.*

Want to get a handle on where you are, emotionally, throughout the course of a day? I challenge you to try a simple experiment.

Stop once an hour to jot down where you are on this scale. Or try it just during the hours you are at work. This will give you a snapshot of where your frame of mind was during that time period.

Your average daily attitude can affect everything that happens to you and everything you do. The good news is, it is something you can examine and think about. It's an opportunity to notice something about a small but important piece of your life.

Let's take a closer look at what you have just done.

1. You directed your thoughts to something you do not normally pay attention to (your relative optimism and pessimism)
2. You noticed extremes in your disposition (negative or positive).
3. You took a practical approach to finding a way to measure those moods (0 to 10 scale)
4. You increased the frequency of your awareness (measuring at each hour for a period of time), and
5. You examined the final result for the day.

Was it tedious? Possibly. Was it scientific? Almost. Did you learn something from it? I'll bet you did.

Why make the effort to do this? By undertaking this experiment, you honed your ability to see something important that you hadn't noticed before.

## The Pitter-Patter of Patterns

Every now and then, life throws us a brand new challenge. But for the most part, we are faced with the same stimuli every day, and we respond to them in pretty much the same ways.

We talked a little bit previously about patterns. Our lives are full of them! Noticing our patterns allows us to begin to see ourselves in new ways.

When we become aware of our patterns, we can have some control over whether we want to keep or change them. Otherwise, the pattern will just be there, doing its thing, day in and day out, affecting your life in ways in which you are unaware. Like the pitter-patter of rain on a metal roof, you notice it at first, but then it disappears into the background, unless you purposely try to pay attention to it again.

Patterns have to do with how you spend your time. Since we all have only a limited amount of time, noticing patterns can help you get the most out of the time you have.

If you begin to observe them, you'll find patterns in sleeping, working, traveling, spending time with family and friends, relaxing, reading, watching TV, social networking, eating, and enjoying your hobbies. In many cases, you'll find you have very specific, automatic patterns that help you in driving to work, balancing the checkbook, taking care of the yard, taking the car in for service, and hundreds more. Just account for how you spend your time, and you'll see patterns, both large and small.

Why is it important to recognize your patterns? So that you can budget your time wisely and spend it doing what you truly want to do. If you don't make conscious choices about how to spend your time, that time will get away from you.

Did you ever spend four hours on Facebook without realizing it, and then wonder where your whole day went? It's happened to all of us. This is why pattern recognition is important. It can help you curb unhealthy habits and allow you to use your time intentionally, for the things that are important to you.

## Perception Is Everything

There are other patterns in our lives that we seldom notice—patterns that are invisible to the outside world, yet that come through in everything we do. These patterns exist in what we think and how we think. These patterns come out of our very being.

Before discussing these invisible patterns further, let me introduce another fundamental concept of this book. We have mentioned it several times already—the act of *noticing.*

To *notice* is to use your senses to become aware of something. Noticing is the result of intentionally focusing your attention in the present moment. What you focus your attention on can be out there in the physical world, or it can be in your mental or emotional worlds.

In other words, noticing is pausing and "looking" at something you normally allow to pass by, something you wouldn't normally perceive. Noticing means seeing what is normally invisible to you.

Here's a great question to ask yourself to help you discern things you have not seen before:

What do I notice about __________?

For example:

- What do I notice about the way he said that?
- What do I notice about the feelings I'm having about this?
- What do I notice about the way people work at my company?
- What do I notice about how I act around my boss/subordinates/colleagues?
- What do I notice about my recent life?

- What do I notice about the pattern of sleep in my life and how it affects my mood?
- What do I notice about the foods I crave?
- What do I notice about how my wife and I interact?
- What do I notice about how I act at work versus at home?

This simple, yet powerful question can uncover your thoughts and bring hidden reality to light. Think about something important in your life and ask yourself the question now.

To *notice* is to awaken the possibility of seeing something new or seeing in a new way. While it's good that your brain tends to limit what you notice—after all, none of us has the capacity to notice *everything*—it is important that you notice certain things. Those are the things that impact your current reality and future potential.

What can you learn from noticing? You can awaken to the simple fact that you usually do *not* see everything, and that you might be missing many important aspects of yourself and life around you.

Every time you notice something that usually goes unnoticed, you have the potential to see in new ways. Seeing just one new and important thing can literally change your life. It can put you on a different and better course for the future.

Noticing brings awareness. Noticing can shift or change perspective. There is much we don't see in life, and there is even more that we don't understand. But when you do come across something you just don't get, think about this: What do I notice about this? If it's something perplexing, what am I missing?

People can be the most puzzling of all. There is much we don't know about others, such as what they are thinking, how they have been conditioned in their life by circumstances and other people, how self-aware they are, and many other such things.

Let's look at an example you might experience. A friend named John has suddenly become distant. You have noticed a change in his behavior, but what do you know about what is really going on with him?

Think of some possibilities. He could be at a rough spot in his life. Maybe something has happened that he's too embarrassed to talk about. Maybe John recently lost his job or is in the process of getting divorced, and it's been tough. Perhaps one of his parents is gravely ill or recently passed. These are only a few of many real-life possibilities.

When it comes to other people, start by knowing that you don't know. Our lack of information about other people can often lead to misunderstanding. Let's say you react to John's distance by thinking, "How rude of him!" If you don't even consider that you don't know the underlying cause of his behavior, you might get this dead wrong.

While it could be true that he is not being very considerate, John might have a very good reason. Or perhaps you're concerned and wonder what is wrong in a genuine and empathetic way. Again, whatever you guess, you could be right or wrong. At the very least, notice when you lack understanding about the reality of his situation.

So why are we talking about this? Because when a friend surprises us, it's a chance to notice something, not just about him, but about ourselves. Ask yourself, "What do I notice about how *I* am reacting to the fact that John seems distant? Am I being judgmental? Am I angry? Am I worried? Do I care? Am I concerned?"

When you notice your reaction, you come to better understand yourself. And a benefit of better understanding ourselves will likely

lead to a better action on our part, and we will creat
in the end.

## Where Logic Ends and the Heart Begins

Do you notice a key to what we are doing to enhance our insight? We're involving more than just our eyesight—and also more than just our minds. We're involving our emotions, which include something many of us refer to as our *heart*.

Many researchers have studied how emotions influence our lives. You may have heard of *emotional intelligence*, which in large part refers to how well we interact with others. Yet, despite all of the available information, most of us remain unaware of how our emotions influence every part of our lives and how they affect the lives of others. To better understand yourself, emotional intelligence is a subject well worth studying.

In the life and leadership coaching professions, one of the ways we help people is by moving them from only *thinking* about things to *experiencing* them. To do this, the person must incorporate the brain, body, and emotions—the entire being.

Real change involves the whole person, not just the ability to think analytically. Emotions provide valuable information outside of cold hard facts. Emotion is where we really live our lives.

We are emotional beings, after all, and to deny that is to deny our humanness. In truth, we are both thinking *and* emotional human beings.

If we see things only with logical thinking, we see narrowly, through blinders, with limited perspective. When we see with our entire being, including our emotions, we see more broadly.

Take another situation that happened to me recently, when I was flooded with emotions. A man came into a rather empty restaurant where my wife and I were having an early dinner, and he asked if I owned a white car of a certain make. I said yes, and he proceeded to tell me he had just backed into it!

Now, my car was less than two months old, and I had intentionally parked in an empty area so as not to get my doors dinged. My first reaction was not pleasant. I thought, *What kind of an idiot would back into a car in a nearly empty area of a parking lot?*

But then it hit me. I had backed into a car before, too, and I wasn't an idiot. The gentleman seemed genuinely sorry. So what could I do? After I calmed down, we exchanged insurance info and obtained a police report to make sure my car would be repaired. Then, when there was nothing left to do, I went back to enjoying dinner with my wife.

Pay particular attention to your *emotional attachment* to whatever happens. Your preconceived notions can get in the way of the truth.

It's not always easy to recognize the reality of a situation, but this is a skill worth working on. By knowing when to curb your emotions and when to use them, you'll be better equipped to handle any situations that arise.

When you notice the emotions involved in what happens, you learn far more about what is happening than when you just see what appears on the surface. It's like the difference between reading a transcript of a meeting and actually being present to witness the enthusiasm, resistance, and commitment of the participants.

The bottom line here is to pay attention to both the facts and the words you hear or read, and also to the tone of voice, the body language, and the atmosphere that exists. The more you consider each encounter with another human being, the more you'll notice how emotions underlie everything. Emotions are vital because they often drive the outcome.

To improve your insight and sense of understanding, it is important to become more self-aware of your emotions and rational thinking by examining your perspectives. Your perspectives can be broadened and increased by noticing the influence of patterns, attitudes, and other people in your life.

We have just scratched the surface of "seeing" in this short chapter. For a deeper dive to further expand this ability, please go to Chapter 5.

## CHAPTER SUMMARY

Seeing is synonymous with awareness and noticing.

- Your *insight* is often distorted by your preconceived ideas or moods.
- You can increase self-awareness by noticing, especially by noticing patterns.
- *Noticing* can put what you see into context.
- Engage all of yourself—your body, mind, and heart—to develop a fuller life.

**Questions and activities to deepen my learning from this chapter:**

- I will notice and name at least two patterns in my life that I had not previously paid attention to. I will start with how I spend my time. I won't judge myself, I'll just notice!
- How would someone who knows me well describe me? What is something important about me that they might miss?

Seeing - noticing { you, others, emotions

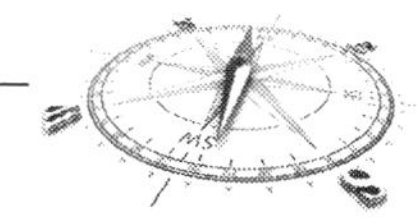

CHAPTER 2

# — THINK —
# I Think Therefore I Am ... a STAR

*"Five percent of the people think;*
*ten percent of the people think they think;*
*and the other eighty-five percent would rather die than think."*
—Thomas A. Edison

For our purposes, *thinking* means *making meaning of what you see.* It also can involve building and expanding upon what you see. So what should you think about?

As a kid I remember playing with building blocks, watching my creations grow taller and taller. My favorite part was pulling out a piece at the bottom and watching my new structure crash to the floor! I learned how important a solid foundation can be.

Much like those building blocks, each of the next three parts of the S.T.A.R. Approach—think, act, reap—requires and builds on the preceding part. In other words, first we *see* something, which allows us to *think* about it. Based on our thoughts, we can take an *action* and *reap* a new result.

It's important to understand that the theme of each section does not stand alone. Instead, what you learn from using this technique is how one idea inevitably leads to the next.

You can't reap if you don't act. You don't want to act if you don't think. (And if you do try to act without thinking, it rarely ends well!) And first, of course, you must see the thing you're thinking about.

In this chapter we add thinking to seeing. We will add the ability to think new thoughts—and to think in new ways—to the awareness we have gained from seeing in new ways. Thinking can be seen as an extension of seeing, allowing us to see deeper, understand more, and better discern what we see, which further helps us see more clearly.

As we begin to see more, we can begin to think in new ways.

Let us begin again with seeing, because if you can't "see" something in your mind's eye, does it even exist? It is outside your realm of consciousness. That which is outside your consciousness goes unnoticed and doesn't enter your thoughts or your life.

Traveling helps open our ways of thinking because it gives us new things to see. When you travel, your eyes can be opened to many things you didn't realize existed before, things you could not experience any other way.

We spent a good part of my childhood in eastern Asia and the Mediterranean, where I learned how different some cultures are from our own. Back in the 1960s I would have never been exposed to foods like boiled octopus and dried squid if I had not lived in Japan. Because I grew up with some very exotic foods, I acquired a taste for dishes that make some Americans squeamish. Having these foods available made them a part of my life.

Then there were the languages. I'll never forget the first time I was at the Paris airport. After living in the Pacific area for nearly nine years, I was suddenly immersed in a world where—although people looked like me and not like Asians—they didn't speak English. I was used to hearing languages such as Japanese, Korean, and Chinese, but hearing a foreign language from Caucasians for the first time was disorienting!

While living in the Mediterranean area for three years, I learned to enjoy hearing Italian, French, Spanish, and North African Arabic. And I got to experience even more new foods. I do love food from the Mediterranean countries!

After being exposed to so much as a child, I continue to have a great deal of appreciation and respect for people from all around the world. Oh, and I continue to love a variety of foods as well!

When we see something we have not seen before, what happens? Well, one option is to allow the thought to pass, which is often what we choose to do. Or we might try to capture the thought, perhaps by writing it down. As the old saying goes, "A short pencil is better than a long memory."

Yet there's a third option, when what we see is of sufficient interest: We can ruminate on it. Most often, when we do this, we do two things: We *deepen* the thought, so it influences other thoughts; and we *expand* the thought, which allows us to see even more. Philosopher L. Mestrius Plutarchus once said, "The mind is not a vessel to be filled, but a fire to be kindled."

Let's look at an example of this. You're walking down the road and meet a homeless man. Your first thought may be that he's a drunkard who deserves to be on the street. But then you notice a tattoo on his arm that shows he's a veteran of war.

Now that you've seen a glimpse of this man's life in that tattoo, you consider that maybe his situation is not as cut-and-dried as you thought. When you talk to him, you discover that war left him with severe PTSD, which makes getting a job difficult.

Now you're thinking about all the other homeless people on the streets who might be suffering from a similar mental illness. What you saw in that tattoo led you to think deeply, to make meaning of what you saw, and to apply those thoughts to other situations. This changed the course of your other assumptions.

Perhaps, as a result, you began volunteering at a homeless shelter and making friends with the people there. And the people you meet there change your worldview—and therefore your life.

The following graphic depicts how the results we reap in the world depend on our actions, which depend on our thinking (meaning making), which comes from what and how we see. Thinking and seeing are internal, while actions provide a bridge between the internal and external. What is received usually manifests outside of our self or creates further thoughts that eventually create something.

The outside results are what we and others often possess or see—but where do the results really come from? They come from inside us. All results stem from our actions and the choices we made because of our thinking.

Until something first occurs inside us, nothing new will be produced that can ultimately be seen outside us in the form of a result.

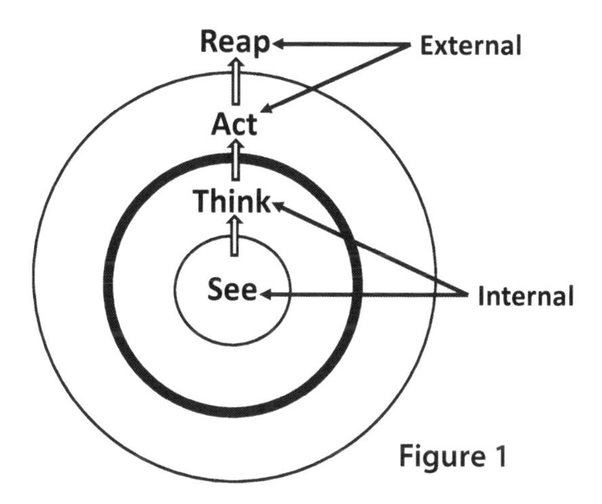


Figure 1

Let's now switch perspectives and look from the outside in. You'll notice that the graphic looks like a target. It is. To win (reap), simply hit the bull's-eye by seeing and developing understanding. Then your actions will become deliberate and produce the best possible result(s). You might see the results on the outside, but they begin on the inside. Whether the result is intangible, such as a relationship, or something material and tangible, it all begins with your seeing something and making meaning of it.

Here's another example. Imagine that the result you want to create is to improve a relationship with a co-worker. The current state of the relationship shows up in the way you interact, and results from what is in you, and what is in the other person.

Right now, the relationship is created by what each of you "see" and how each of you interpret or think about what you see. If you want to change the relationship, what can you do?

You might attempt to change the other person. You might try to get them to see what you want them to see—but this approach usually doesn't work. Experience tells us this is a very difficult path to take in any relationship.

You might look inside yourself at what you see, which his likely limited, and begin working to "see" something else—something new. From there, you can learn a new perspective.

Let's say you look inward and develop more compassion for the other person. You realize he's under a lot of stress with his work, or maybe family issues are weighing on him. As you begin to see him differently, and give it thought, your actions toward him will most likely change, and the resulting interactions will take on a different tone. This process might take the relationship to a new place.

We can continue to use this formula of "seeing" more, then making meaning of our thoughts about what we see, and then behaving (taking action) in a new way.

I once had a strained relationship with a colleague. All I had seen in him was what I considered selfishness. Everything he said was about him and how much success he had or what he wanted. He never took time to listen to much of what I had to say.

Over time my connection to this man irritated me to no end—until one day, something happened. He happened to mention something about his dad, and I noticed he got a little choked up. I started to become curious and question my thoughts about him.

Maybe he'd had a tough life. Maybe he was somewhat insecure in his position and was overcompensating. When I stopped to think about it, I saw *myself* in him, to a degree. Although I had become tired of listening to this man talk about himself, I decided to make myself available to hear more.

Sure enough, as he slowly opened up, I discovered he'd had a chaotic childhood and an abrasive yet mostly absent father. I started to feel more compassion toward him. He had struggled to finish school and was not as confident as I had thought. His cockiness was an act he put on to cover his insecurities.

As I came to understand him differently, our relationship changed, and we became good friends. I was able to give him some positive input and reinforcement—and he seemed to change right before my eyes into a man I had not known before.

Nothing in the world that I said would have made him change. Instead, the way I treated him helped us both change. To this day he is a good friend and calls me for advice because he knows I care and will encourage him. Out of a strained work relationship, a wonderful friendship emerged. And it only happened because I chose to see him in a different way—as a human being instead of as an obstacle in my life.

Now let's look at creating something tangible. We're going to analyze something so deeply, we will know how to make it into a business. Choose a product, any product. Starting with what you know and see, ask yourself, "What else would I need to know in order to produce and successfully sell this product?"

As you consider and do your research, some discovery will take place to allow you to see more and understand more. Begin asking questions about what these things might be. Do you know how customers will receive this new product? To do so, you'll need to become more informed about what customers want and will accept.

Can you make a profit from this item? To learn that, you'll need a better understanding of how much it will cost to produce the new product. Once you understand the costs, you can begin to move forward, taking action to obtain what you need.

Only when you have gone through these steps—first seeing, then understanding, and finally taking action—can you reap results. Those results will further inform what you "see."

Perhaps you'll see that the price needs to be dropped, or that the product needs to be adjusted to make customers happier. This cycle continues until you clearly understand what is needed. From that point on, you can become deliberate about what action to take to produce the results you want.

Thomas Edison had to go through this process when he was perfecting the lightbulb. (Yes, he perfected it. He didn't invent it. The lightbulb was invented many decades before by such people as Sir Humphry Davy, who connected a battery—which he developed—to a piece of carbon.)

Edison approached his vision with a thirst for knowledge. He could clearly see what he wanted, and he came to understand what it would take to make electricity possible for home use: a central power station and a network of wires that would extend to individual households. After all, what good would a lightbulb be on a large scale if power and wires were not in place?

It took Edison more than his famous 1,000 experiments to find exactly the right combination of bulb, vacuum, and filament. He also had to think beyond that to see what was needed to generate electricity, and how to wire a city to bring light to the masses.

What do you see and have a passion for that might change the world—or at least *your* world?

As Scripture says, "Where there is no vision, the people perish." When you can't see, you can't create anything. What you can't see doesn't *exist* (to you).

Instead, you have an inherent curiosity that responds to questions, which urge your brain to grow.

Ask questions of yourself and your world, as often as you can. It will increase your understanding of how your brain works and can greatly enhance your life. If you don't ask questions about yourself, you're leading an *unexamined life*—and as the ancient philosopher Socrates stated, "The unexamined life is not worth living." While harsh, there is an element of truth to this statement.

Think about this: The quality of a question determines the quality of the learning. Or put another way, the more powerful the question, the greater the potential to expand your understanding. So how do we ask more powerful questions? Here are some rules of thumb:

**The least powerful questions** are closed-ended and result in a simple answer like *yes or no*, or ask you to make a simple choice—such as, *Is this better than that?* These questions usually begin with the words *who, when, where,* or *which.*

Low-power questions generally lead to short, defined answers, and often lead the person to a reaction or response. They can be great for narrowing down and bringing out more succinct answers; however, they can miss a tremendous amount of valuable information that lies in the deeper layers of truth.

**Powerful questions** most often begin with *what* or *how.* These questions often lead to more profound insight and reflection. Powerful questions can bring answers that supply flavor and richness, getting us to think more deeply and to look inside ourselves.

It's more difficult to ask a powerful question, but the effort can pay huge dividends. Being willing to phrase and consider powerful questions will help you gain new perspectives, and help you learn and grow.

Powerful questions are important both when you ponder your own life and when you speak to others. Instead of asking simple questions like, "Do you like this?" ask "What do you like best about this?" Instead of asking "Where do you come from?" ask "What made you decide to move here?" The latter questions will provide far more insight into the person, because you'll get a deeper layer of information.

The most powerful questions begin with *why*. *Why* questions can be powerful when used correctly, yet they should be used carefully. When asking someone else "why," you're asking for a motive or underlying principle, and that can seem judgmental.

I encourage you to ask "Why did you do that?" *of yourself* to help probe your underlying assumptions. Yet ask that of someone else, and you're putting that person on the spot in a way that can be most uncomfortable!

*Why* questions for other people might be best rephrased as *how* or *what* questions. Instead of "Why did you do that?" you can ask "What happened?" or "How did you come to that decision?" Those questions ask for tangible specifics, and people are more likely to have the answers readily available.

While a *why* question can be useful when we are looking inward, when directed at others, we should first notice our own intent by asking "Why am I asking this question? What do I need to know? Can I ask a question that will give me the same information without seeming judgmental?"

Try this effective exercise to better understand yourself. Ask yourself the same *why* question multiple times. For example, "Why did I do it?" Or perhaps "Why haven't I done it yet?" After your first answer to the question you choose, ask it again of your answer—"But why?" Then ask again and again until you have mined all that can be said. It will astound you how much deeper you can go when you do this, and how many layers you can unravel.

Following is a quick reference showing questions and their relative strength.

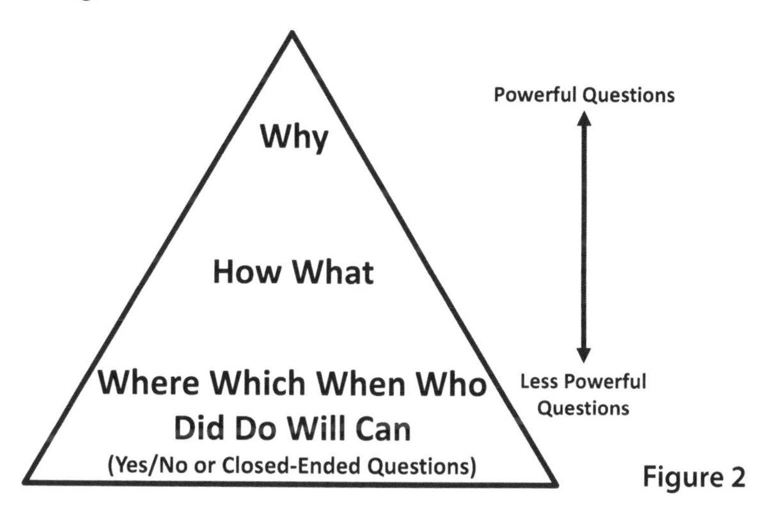


Figure 2

While all types of questions are important, to begin to expand our understanding, it is helpful to start with the more probing questions and follow with the rest to fill in specifics. As an example, let's take an inquiry about someone's life: "What do you want?"

Now, you could add more to that question, but I find that the shorter the question, the richer the answer. If you asked, "What is it you want in life?" or "When do you want to start living?" you will likely get a totally different answer. Should you ask a similar question using *who, where, when,* or *which,* you will likely receive a short answer that will not aid your exploration of the subject or fuel your curiosity as much as if you ask a *what* or *how* question.

Answer the following questions for yourself to see how the answers differ. This time, let's use the subject of your job.

- Where do I want to work?
- When do I want to work?
- Who do I want to work with?
- Which organization do I want to work for?
- Would I prefer to work for myself or run my own business?

Each of these would likely produce a short response. Then ask the following:

- What do I want from my work?
- How can I get more from my job?
- What would success look like at work?

Remember: The *least powerful* questions provide the least information, such as yes, no, the location, a name, and so on.

Since asking questions is critical to your growth, let's recap and go a little deeper into each type of question.

**Low-power** questions usually start with *where, which, when, who, do, will,* or *can* and can provide information, although it is often limited.

**More powerful** questions usually start with *how* or *what,* and give you a deeper level of insight into the situation at hand. These questions require the answerer to actually think.

It's important to ask powerful questions of yourself because they lead to introspection and reflection, which expand your brain power.

**Powerful questions** often lead to discovery and understanding, literally opening and expanding the mind. You can usually follow up with an open-ended question like "and what else?" to dig even deeper.

The most powerful questions usually begin with *why*.

- "Why did you do that?"
- "Why do you feel this way?"
- "Why don't you make another choice?"

Returning to our example of asking someone about work, interviewers often ask, "Why do you want to work here?" The question can sound judgmental, putting an emphasis on the "here" rather than the "why."

To adjust the tone, we might ask "Why is work important to you?" because the answer is broader in its implication. How you phrase the question is important, and where you place the inflection with your voice can change the meaning.

As a little exercise, ask "Why would you want to work there?" with someone, putting a stronger emphasis on different words in the sentence, asking yourself how each version would make someone feel (being criticized, judged, neutral, or other).

While *why* questions are considered the most powerful, they can be like using a sledgehammer to drive a tack at times because of their potential critical or judgmental nature. Depending on the situation, a why question can make a person shut down.

When we feel judged—and especially if we're being asked something for which we don't yet have an answer—our emotional reaction can affect our ability to think rationally. Trying to answer the wrong "why" question can cause us to enter a fight, freeze, or flight mode.

For this reason, using "why" to start a question is often avoided in professions such as coaching. As a coach, we wish to expand, not contract, thinking.

Just keep in mind that "why" questions are powerful, and use them in a way that is helpful, not harmful. Don't ask *why* unless you can do so without judgement or sounding critical.

Want to know a little secret you can use to empower your questions? Develop a deep, genuine interest in whatever the topic the person of whom you are asking a question. The more you are about something, the greater the potential to develop better and more powerful questions.

Like many things we do in life, learning to ask powerful questions is a skill, and genuine curiosity will help us to grow in the skill and to enjoy developing it. Without sincere interest, there is little incentive to endure the discomfort that sometimes accompanies asking the questions that can change your, or another person's, life.

One last thought about questions: They help us prepare for learning and growth, and for making decisions about next steps. The more prepared we are, the more opportunities we see.

As Roman philosopher Seneca said, millennia ago: "Luck is what happens when preparation meets opportunity." In other words, the more you prepare, the more likely you'll get "lucky" when an opportunity comes along. (To others, you may appear lucky—but your achievements will have come from preparing yourself well before the opportunity arises.)

It all begins with asking the right questions to help you think new thoughts.

As you continue your journey through this book, work on asking yourself powerful questions. I assure you, the rewards will be great! As Merilee Adams of the Inquiry Institute wrote, "Change your questions, change your life!"

## What Is the Question?

Let's say you find yourself in the situation where you feel stuck in life. You sense there might be more for you "out there" somewhere, but you have no idea how to get there. How can questions help?

First, practice your questioning skills. Start with something that truly interests you. Focus on a subject and use questions to explore it as fully as possible.

Some years ago, I had the responsibility of turning around a company. Since the company was losing a great deal of money, my first question was, "What do I need to know?" This led me on a search to understand where the company was, how it got there, what was currently happening, and what might be possible to fix it.

During my investigation, many other questions surfaced, which led me to a deeper and more thorough understanding of the root issues. This set us up to make better decisions to obtain the best and quickest results possible—and we turned that company around. It felt like quite an accomplishment! It's one thing to just focus on cutting losses, but quite another to change direction while eliminating losses and producing greater results.

Now think about anything you have interest in, such as a hobby. I love photography and because of my passion for taking pictures, I have learned a great deal about cameras, lenses, and light. There is so much to learn and so many new things happening in photography that it has been a lifelong learning experience for me, and one that I enjoy greatly. There's always some new innovation in equipment or technique that spurs my interest.

What continues to capture your interest, and how much more could you learn about it if you kept asking questions?

You may have noticed that one question leads to another question, which leads to more questions. A good question often does that, especially if it is an area that intrigues you. A good question will open you to new thoughts and understanding, unearthing more areas to explore.

These new thoughts and greater understanding will, of course, lead to even more queries, and so the cycle continues. (Notice Figure 3 and the see-think cycle in the middle of the graphic.)

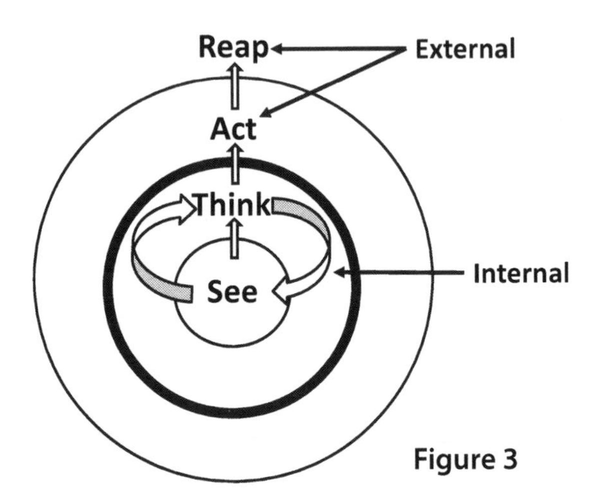


Figure 3

As you can *see* (pun intended!), good and powerful questions are critical to expanding our knowledge base. As we expand our knowledge, we **See** opportunities we might have otherwise missed. We can then **Think** to thoughtfully make better choices and **Act** on them to **Reap** results that would not have happened otherwise.

As you might have noticed already, this is the foundation of the S.T.A.R. pattern: seeing in new ways, thinking new thoughts, taking new actions, and reaping new results.

If you want to create a life that is full of purpose and meaning, fulfilling and rewarding, learn to ask questions and follow them up with more questions!

## I Think I Can, I Think I Can

A little tip here—don't be too concerned about questions that may lead you to worry about what you *can't* do. These thoughts will inevitably arise in you or in others. Get to the root of your belief; either you believe you *can* or you believe you *can't*. If you are in the latter camp, look more deeply. Question that assumption. Never give up. You can change your beliefs, including those in yourself!

Whenever you focus on limitations and about what you can't do or have, it limits or derails your ability to create something new, better, greater. To a large degree, these are actually self-limiting beliefs. Yes, you read that correctly. They are limits you put on yourself! They are limits you inadvertently choose to accept.

Turn the focus away from what you or they **can't** do and toward what you **can** do. Whenever the thought "I can't do that!" comes up, stop and ask, "So, what *can* I do?"

I often stop and mentally shift myself or my client 180 degrees, and ask, "What *can* I/you/we do?" When asked such a question, you will naturally seek an answer. The results are often surprising.

While working with a leader whose company was stuck from moving forward after zero growth for several years, he took to heart that it was useless to focus on what he and his people can't do. After a few short months of coaching, he finally made the transition to turn off the *can'ts* and turn on the *cans*. He had been steeped in so many years of hearing what he couldn't do that when he finally began asking what he could do and what his people could do, a major shift occurred in the company. Yes, there were still the naysayers, but the result of this small change in thinking became the turning point for the company. As they had more and more successes, they were able to put the company onto the growing and profitable course it is on today. Was it easy? No. But his persistence in learning to focus on the *can* instead of the *can't* made all the difference in the world to the company.

The process behind refocusing the direction of your thoughts to what you *can* do is simple, yet the solution is not always easy. Take this one step at a time.

It's well documented that your mind can only deal with one thought at a time. When we attempt to multi-task, such as thinking about what we can and can't do, we switch back and forth between the *can* and the *can't*, restricting the full use of our brain on one thing, and that can limit the quality of our thinking.

So once you've said you can't do something, put that thought aside. Focus fully on the opposite—what you *can* do. When we choose to think about what we *can* do in a given situation, we focus our energy on creating what we want, and we move toward what we want.

I am not saying you should continue to ignore the current reality of a situation; however, what we perceive as reality is often incomplete anyway, and only a small part of the bigger whole. It's safe to put it aside for a while.

For example, let's say I did a lot of research on a specific car I wanted. I go to a car dealer and realize the price tag is more than I want to pay. I say to myself, "Wow, this car costs more than I want to spend. As much as I want it, I can't justify spending that much money." This is my reality at that point.

I can stand there and believe I can't afford it and go away disappointed. Or perhaps, I can ask myself a question: "What do I really want?" and "What *can* I do?"

In researching the car, I've uncovered a great deal about what I want. I really like the styling, the leather interior, and the way the car handles and drives. On an emotional level, I have my "heart set" on this car. (Emotions, by the way, not logic, drive most of our buying decisions.)

Now, as I exit the showroom, feeling disheartened, I look over at a row of used cars. There I notice the same car—virtually identical but two years older. It's even in the color I want!

I turn around and go back into the showroom and ask the salesperson, "How much is that diamond white car?" She gets the price for me, which is considerably less than the new car. It has very few miles on it, and it's in excellent condition inside and out. It has every option I want and more. I begin to get excited again.

I usually purchase new cars and it seems a bit of a letdown. But it sure is a great car ... and it's one I can more easily afford.

This actually happened to me some years back. While a car should not be an impulse buy for most of us, it can be a very emotional purchase.

In my car-shopping experience, I shifted my perspective from that of wanting a new car to realizing there are some reliable used vehicles available, many like new, with excellent warranties. And the savings can be significant. That day, my range of choices widened considerably.

Here's another example of what changing a *can't* to a *can* will do.

Many years ago, a young man began working his way up the ladder in his field, yet he lacked the college degree that most people had for similar positions. He had gone into military service straight out of high school and married very young, and had a child. Now he spent all his free time going to night college. What he really wanted was to run a company someday.

He could have said, "Why bother going after my dream when I don't have the requisite education? Most people with such a job have a master's degree, and I'm still struggling to get my bachelor's."

He could have thought, "There's just no way; I can't do it. I'm not qualified." Yet he was a hard worker and had more than enough intelligence to run a company and do it well. In fact, he excelled at everything he did, from operations to sales and marketing, to full-charge management.

He did so well that most people had no idea he lacked a formal college degree, and it didn't hold him back—yet he always struggled internally with the fact that he hadn't finished college.

He continued to work hard and get promotions. Sure, he had doubts at times, but he came to believe he could actually run a company, and he didn't let the *can't* stop him. Eventually, he held the top marketing and technical position in the largest company in his industry.

Later, he ran some large companies as president and CEO. He was in high demand as both an internal and external consultant, and was awarded several patents—despite the fact that he never finished his bachelor's degree!

In case you're wondering, that man was me. I've spent much of my life believing I *can* do practically anything I put my mind to, and helping others come to believe in themselves. In fact, I later obtained a professional coaching certification from Duquesne University in Pittsburgh and then taught a leadership course in Shanghai, China, for Duke University.

During my career, I've had quite a few employees who had master's degrees and some who had PhDs. My success depended little on my education level and very much on my beliefs.

As Henry Ford once said, "Whether you think you can, or you think you can't—you're right."

What are your beliefs about what you can or can't do?

I'm sure you could add such examples from your past experiences if you think about it. We often see reality only in part, and the more we realize this truth, the more we explore. The more we explore, the more options we will find, and the better our chances of success.

Being curious and asking questions will expand your ability to see more, leading you to more options, which will lead to having more choices on which to act, allowing you to reap different results. There's that familiar pattern again!

## It's All a Matter of Perspective

If you've ever watched *The Matrix*, the premise revolves around a society that lives in a reality that doesn't exist. They go about their lives unaware that what they think is real is, in fact, an illusion.

While we might not live in a matrix controlled by energy-sucking robots, one aspect of the movie rings true for many of us: What we think we see isn't always what it seems.

It's always important to remember that what we see might not be accurate, which can limit our ability to think. In fact, we may be not seeing some things at all. It can be helpful to broaden your perspective so you see more. Perspective is limited by what we don't see and what we don't know.

Once you see and understand more, your thinking can change. I know, change is difficult, and many people are resistant to change. But remember the Matrix: To view things through a limited perspective is limiting, perhaps even blinding.

To a person who doesn't like to deal with numbers, looking at a profit and loss (P&L) statement and balance sheet of a company can be overwhelming. Unless you have a background in this kind of information, it won't make much sense.

I recall the first time I was exposed to P&L statements; were it not for some accounting courses in college, I would have been totally lost in attempting to understand them. Because I had so little experience reading a P&L and balance sheet, I didn't completely comprehend what they presented, and I actually considered them a waste of time!

Since I had come up through the ranks, I believed the *real* part of the business was out there in production and sales—not in a bunch of numbers that the "bean counters" came up with.

Of course, over time, my perspective shifted considerably. As I advanced into upper management, I learned how these statements could inform me of different aspects about the business, and how important they really are.

Looking back, it's hard to admit how I was so resistant to such a wealth of information, which I now know is vital to running a large company.

Let's look at some other perspective shifts we have already been through. As a child, we could see very little outside of our small world. The world was all about us and our needs. Then we entered school, and throughout the school years, we had regular perspective shifts as we learned and matured.

When we went off after high school to college or to work, our perspectives broadened even more. We could now see many things we hadn't even considered when we were younger. We found out the world was about much more than our immediate needs. Then our appreciation of other people expanded tremendously.

As young adults, things like dating, driving a car, earning a paycheck, choosing the beginning of a course for life, marriage, children, saving for retirement, and so on became realities in our lives. If our perspectives did not continue to grow, change, and shift as we aged, we could not have matured.

So why do so many people eventually stop growing? As we age, we become more set in our ways. We unconsciously choose to limit our perspectives in many areas of life, so we can be more comfortable in knowing what we already know. When we stop learning, we stop growing. We quit exploring, preferring to maintain the status quo.

Are you stagnant or are you growing? How do you see yourself? Others? Their opinions? Are you stuck in some areas of your thinking? Perhaps some exploration into your existing perspectives and your willingness to change them will help you answer these questions.

## Greater Perspective, Greater Possibilities

This brings us to another noteworthy point as we develop our thoughts. There is nearly always *more than one* perspective we can take about anything in life. Just when we think we have thought about a subject completely, another viewpoint emerges that changes our perspective! Have you had this experience?

Each new perspective opens our minds to seeing more possibilities, enhancing and expanding our understanding of reality, and unearthing opportunities.

The easiest and greatest way to expand your perspective is by simply getting input from others with different points of view (perspectives) and by asking them powerful questions.

Did you ever meet someone who enlarged your thinking? It happens all the time in conversations and meetings.

How does it happen? When we hear a different point of view, we will either accept it in part, or in whole, or we will dismiss it. Whenever we come to understand a different perspective, even a little, our thinking shifts and can be enlarged.

Asking someone their viewpoints on a subject is, in fact, the easiest way to broaden your perspective—provided you keep an open mind.

An example of this is when we look at political issues, which can be polarizing. We may be absolutely positive that our opinion is the only one that is correct or accurate. Yet another person may have completely contrary views.

That's one of the great things about the human race—we are not all clones, nor should we be. Each of us has unique experiences, backgrounds, trials, and tribulations that have made us who we are. Imagine a world without the variety that differences in people creates. It would be very boring, to say the least.

Try a little experiment. Find someone with a different position on a subject and ask them questions about their views, in a genuinely curious, sincere, nonthreatening way. The only agenda here is to learn, not to convince them of anything. Don't try to persuade them to your viewpoints; simply become curious and ask sincere questions about the subject and their thoughts on it. Then listen. You may be surprised by what you learn.

I once worked with a man named Joe who had different religious views than my friend Tom (one was Catholic, the other Protestant). Whenever Joe and Tom discussed religion, the conversation would grow heated and contentious. I recall one of them often becoming so frustrated with the other that he would literally turn red in the face, his veins ready to pop!

Rather than get tangled up in their conversations, I became curious about their beliefs. I started asking a lot of questions about what they believed and how they had come to those beliefs. It amazed me how well they each knew the Scriptures. We had some very interesting conversations.

I discovered that both of their beliefs were more closely aligned than I had originally thought. To this day the three of us can speak openly about our beliefs. Now, we tend to focus on what we have in common rather than what we differ on.

Furthermore, my entire perspective on what I thought I knew about their faith changed. Instead of criticizing their beliefs, I developed a profound respect for each man.

Since life is about relationships, one of the great things about asking powerful questions of others or yourself is they can open our minds to see new and fresh perspectives, and to understand more of what actually exists. This allows us to see more possibilities, leading to greater opportunities.

In addition to getting other people's perspectives, it is rather easy to dig into your own thoughts and develop different perspectives by simply asking yourself questions. Coaches do this all the time with their clients.

Start by writing down your initial viewpoint on a subject. Then shoot for at least six to eight additional views. Begin by asking yourself questions like: "What's another viewpoint?" "What am I leaving out?" "What would (name of person) say about this?" "What else?" and so on. The trick is to examine the subject from as many viewpoints as you can come up with, which will greatly enhance your overall perspective on a given issue. Try this with anything that is on your mind, but especially with something that you have a strong opinion about. See what happens. Your subject could be a person, an object, a place, a philosophy, or anything at all.

What possibility exists in asking ourselves more powerful questions? What indeed! In Section 3 of this book, you will find **Exercise 1**, entitled "Developing Greater Perspective." This is a simple exercise that will quickly show you how to expand your perspective on a given subject, leading to better understanding, more possibilities, and more choices on which to act.

The example shown is on the subject of saving for retirement, based on coaching a forty-four-year-old business professional. I urge you to review the exercise and apply it to something in your own life.

## The Either/Or, Both/And Conundrum

Let's discuss one final topic that can help us think more fully and deeply about thinking: changing the hard line we often draw when we see things as black or white. What about the numerous shades of gray? What if *both* sides of an issue are true?

If something is either this way or that, with no other options, are we really seeing clearly? Perhaps, but perhaps not.

For example, can you work or not work and still make a living? Well, it depends, doesn't it? Most of us are gainfully employed at some point in our lives—yet you don't work *all* of the time, do you? There's plenty of in-between time.

You can run into problems when you allow your work to consume your life. I've been there. During much of my career, I thought the businesses I worked in couldn't get along without me giving 110 percent, all the time. I rarely took vacations, at the expense of spending time with my family.

Before I knew it, my daughter was off to college, and we were empty nesters. Wow, did that time go too fast! Looking back, I could have done things far differently. Yet what is past is past. We can't change what was, but we can learn valuable lessons from it.

One day, I had a wakeup call. The president of the company I worked for at the time was transferred back to the main HQ in Europe, and we kept in touch, as good friends do. He was a few years older than me.

One day, he said, "You know, Bill, all of the years I've worked and all of the sacrifices I've made, rarely taking my vacation time, I was losing time with my family. Not one person ever thanked me for being so dedicated."

By then, I was reconsidering a lot of things in my life and realized that was true for me, too. All the years of sacrificing for my job at the expense of my family, and not one person had ever thanked me for my dedication or "sacrifice"!

In fact, no one had ever asked me or my friend to do what we did. We just assumed we *had* to do it, because that's what others did. My assumption was directing my life. How wrong we were!

I could have worked hard *and* taken time off to not work. I could have seen my work-life balance as both/and, rather than either/or. Either work or not, or both work and not. That simple change in my thinking set me on a new course.

What can you do when faced with an either/or type of situation? Ask the simple question: "Is this really a this-or-that, exclusively one or the other? Is it *really* a black-or-white situation?"

Then ask, "What could make it *both of these,* or a this-*and*-that situation?"

You will certainly find many opportunities to apply this question in life. Just remember, not everything is as clearly defined as it appears on the surface.

Take, for example, when you retire. Will you retire and not work anymore? Really? That is one way to look at it. But what if you took on a different view? What if you considered retiring as only doing what you want when it comes to work?

In that situation, you might not work at all—or you might decide, after some time, that you'd like to do a few things, as I have. I continue to coach because I enjoy helping other people—yet I tremendously enjoy being retired and the free schedule it allows me.

As I often say, "In retirement, every day is Saturday, except Sunday." My work-life balance now is one of both/and, not either/or. I've proven to myself that you can have your cake and eat it too!

In Chapter 6, you will find more great ideas on how to expand the way you think and how to think in new ways.

## CHAPTER SUMMARY

- Each step of the S.T.A.R. model builds on the p piece and also feeds back into it. Seeing enables thinking, which will broaden and deepen the understanding of what you see.
- Assumptions affect how and what you see, often acting as blinders, limiting and holding you back—or even completely blinding you!
- Questions facilitate the depth and quality of learning.
- The least powerful questions are closed-ended, Yes or No questions. Powerful questions are open-ended, often starting with "How" or "What." The most powerful of all questions start with "Why?"
- Focus on what you CAN DO in any given situation, not what you cannot do.
- Greater perspective will allow you to explore greater possibilities.
- Instead of settling for *either/or*, find the *both/and* possibility.

**Questions and activities to deepen my learning from this chapter:**

- Why is it important to hone my ability to ask powerful questions?
- I will practice asking a variation of the same question, using each of the three levels from the least to the most powerful questions.
- I will perform **Exercise 1 - Developing Greater Perspective in Section 3**, choosing a topic that is very important to me.
- What three questions could someone ask me that would give them a deeper understanding of me?

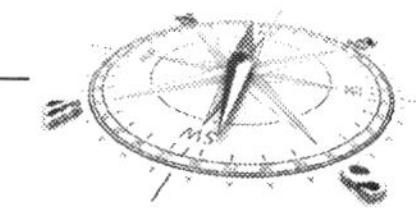

CHAPTER 3

# — ACT —
# Aaannnd ... Action!

*"Don't wait for things to happen. Make them happen."*
—Roy Bennett

As you continue to focus and enhance your vision so you can see more, allowing you to think more fully—and in new and different ways—you will discover more (and better) options on which to act. As we delve into this section, we will continue to build on seeing new things that allow us to think new thoughts so that we can take new actions to reap new results. That's how you become a STAR! Let's dive straight in.

## So what, now what?

Every time you observe something, you can ask yourself two questions: So what? And now what?

at?" asks you to think about what you have seen. "So ...ans, what does this have to do with my life, or the bigger picture of things? "Now what?" is equivalent to: What am I going to DO about this?

Considering each of us has the same amount of time in a day, and that time is such a precious resource, exactly what we decide to do with our time determines what we reap in life.

Think of it this way: The effort we put forth, or don't put forth, during a given period of time *always* produces a result. If you plant your garden and put the effort into tending it, you'll produce delicious vegetables. If, however, you don't put in any effort and neglect your garden, you'll produce a scraggly, pest-filled heap of weeds.

"Now what?" asks: What do you want to do in the time you have available?

Do you make a deliberate decision each day on what you will spend your time and energy doing? Or do your days just "sort of happen?" Without understanding what is most important to us, our days are going to happen anyway.

Most of us attempt to take on many tasks in a day, some intentionally, some not so intentionally. Nonetheless, we will "spend" the day on something. The better you learn to manage your time, the more benefits you will reap.

Let's look quickly at three things that will help you ACE your time-management practices:

- Attention
- Choice
- Effort

Let's start with the basics: what you notice. Where you place your attention determines what you see, think, take action on, and reap results from. What is your attention on today?

The list of things you pay attention to will present you with choices. When you *choose* to do something and commit to seeing it through, you can accomplish it. Think about how well you've been handling these choices. What choices did you make yesterday with your time and talents? What do you choose to accomplish today?

Once your attention has focused you, and you've committed to a choice, all that's left is to *act* by exerting effort. In other words, just do it! What do you choose to do today? Not what will you "try to do," but what will you actually *do?* Inaction is a zero-sum choice. You either jump off the diving board or you don't.

Sounds simple, doesn't it? Let's take a closer look at these parts of time management: attention, choice, and effort.

So many things vie for our attention. Here we sit, working away on a report, when the phone rings, an email comes in, someone stops in to ask a question or just to chat, and on and on come the interruptions. When we resume our work, it is difficult to pick up where we left off, and it takes a while to get back to where we were, in order to make progress.

And so the day goes. And the week. And the month. You get the idea ... Over time, it seems we worked hard, yet accomplished little for the time spent. Such is the way time flows in far too many of our lives. The funny thing about time is, it is always flowing, never ceasing. Whether it's working for us or not, there it goes!

In addition to outside interruptions, we also create *our own* interruptions. The ability to focus can vary, day by day, even hour by hour. If it weren't so, accomplishing things would be far easier.

We would tackle a project and finish it in "one fell swoop." But in real life, we attempt to tackle not one, or two, or three, but several things in a day—and if we're really lucky, we might complete one of these tasks.

Interruptions are costly, yet they are a fact of life. Numerous studies have shown it takes time to get back to where you left off. In fact, a University of California Irvine study claims it takes nearly twenty-five minutes to resume where we were when interrupted—and those minutes are a high cost to pay. That can add up to serious time lost, given how many interruptions can happen during a day.

We can't work in a bubble, isolated from all interruptions. But we can be intentional about where we focus (and refocus) our attention. Some good questions to ask yourself regularly during any given day are:

- Am I spending *this moment* doing something that will make a meaningful difference?
- Where am I placing my attention?
- How can I block out interruptions?

We just said that you can't block out interruptions completely—but you can certainly try to cut down on the things that intrude on your space and waste your time! Here are a few simple things I have found to be valuable in increasing my ability to focus my attention and get things done:

- Turn off my cell phone.
- Put my phone on do not disturb.
- Turn off all email and social apps notifications.
- Block out chunks of time on my calendar and stick to the "work appointments" I set.

- Close the office door for one hour (or more) and see what I can get done in that period of uninterrupted work time.
- Put up a DO NOT DISTURB sign.
- Never, ever attempt to multitask on anything of importance.

The last item, *multitasking*, is of key importance. David Rock, in his excellent book *Your Brain at Work*, says multitasking doesn't pay and isn't actually even *possible*. Or check out Sue Shellenbarger's *Wall Street Journal* article entitled, "Multitasking Makes You Stupid: Studies Show Pitfalls of Doing Too Much at Once."

When you try to split your focus among two or more tasks, not only does it lower your IQ, it also greatly slows your ability to get things done. Your poor brain, which can focus on only one thing at a time, is forced to switch back and forth between tasks—and that greatly diminishes your ability to make decisions about either project.

According to the American Psychological Association, "task-switching" reduces productivity by 40 percent, because it takes time to reconnect with what you were working on when interrupted—even if you caused the interruption yourself.

Most of us lose 28 percent of our productive working time—that's more than two hours!—each day because of constant interruptions and recovery time! And I believe that is a very conservative estimate of time lost.

Think of this: You've met with several people to make a decision about something important. Some of you are talking about the decision, but others are constantly checking phones, replying to emails, or doing something else.

Not only will the distracted attendees potentially miss something of importance in the meeting, or miss their opportunity to participate—but those emails they send might be riddled with mistakes!

And this doesn't even account for the disrespect being shown to everyone else at the meeting by those who are failing to focus fully. If you were running the meeting, wouldn't you want everyone's attention on the task at hand?

As it is, too much time is wasted in meetings. Attempting to multitask wastes even more precious minutes. Although it's becoming more common to see people looking at their phones *all the time,* wouldn't you feel frustrated by the distractions of attendees' phones, tablets, or computers?

Let's say you are working on a project that should take one hour to complete if your sole focus is on the project. What is the likelihood of finishing within that hour if you stop to check your email or suddenly try to focus on something else, even for just a few minutes? Be honest with yourself about how many distractions you add into your own life, and how it affects your productivity.

Just test this concept in your own life. Put your phone in the other room, ringer off, when you begin a task. I'm sure you can easily *more than double* your productivity just by focusing your attention on the matter at hand and controlling or avoiding distractions. You'll be giving yourself something of immense value: the value of your time.

## 3x5 Cards and ACE

Some years back, I learned a lesson that I've applied in my own life and in working with young professionals I have mentored over the years. It's a relatively simple system. At the beginning of each day, we would write tasks we wanted to finish that day on a 3x5 index card, dating it at the top.

If you're curious as to why we used 3x5 index cards, it was mostly happenstance. I've used 3x5 cards for years to make notes on because they're inexpensive, they fit easily into a pocket, and they're durable. They're also easy to store and sort, which is helpful if you decide to go back through a stack to analyze and notice patterns. For people who process information visually, the "low-tech" cards might work better than note apps or spreadsheets.

So, now you have a portable little "To Do" list. At the end of the day, or the next morning, we would cross off any tasks that were completed. We then would carry unfinished tasks over to the card for the next day, and sometimes add another item or two.

I urged the people I mentored to create daily cards for a few weeks. What did we learn from doing this simple exercise? Well, it wasn't pretty …

Examining the stack of index cards that had accumulated during a week or a month was extremely revealing. Despite our best efforts, we found we crossed off few items—far too few—and left many undone tasks remaining.

If someone finished just one major task in a day, it was cause for celebration. Completing two or three major tasks was considered a huge victory! Unfortunately, because we needed to add more items or tasks to the daily lists—and usually ended up carrying them over to the next day—our lists continued to grow. Looking at a longer list every day was most discouraging.

Then we hit on the idea to put *only the most important* things on the cards. To make the list, we would ask some qualifying questions:

1. Is this item one of the top five things I must complete today, in whole or in part?
2. What will the impact of completing this task be a year from now?
3. How does this task fit with my vision and purpose in life?

The first question narrowed our list down considerably. This step was especially important, because we were lucky to cross one or two items off the list each day.

The second and third questions helped us put the task in perspective with the bigger picture. Minor tasks were quickly eliminated when we realized they wouldn't matter in a year or didn't align with our biggest goals.

We no longer carried minor tasks over, as with a traditional list. Instead, we added them to a separate running to-do list.

Now to be clear, we only put *major* tasks we needed to accomplish on the daily card—tasks that were meaningful and that enhanced our results and our future. But that meant our cards were no longer comprehensive guidelines for how to spend each minute of the day.

For example, checking email consumes large amounts of time and energy. It's important that it be done at regular intervals, but it's not a major task that would make the 3x5 card daily list. Attending an important decision-making meeting would be on the 3x5 card, yet attending an informal planning meeting might not.

What about those brief interactions with our coworkers? Relationships with others are a very important part of our work and our lives, but they wouldn't make the list—and they also can consume a huge amount of time.

Many aspects of life require our time and are important, in addition to the specific tasks or projects we must complete. While we can't overlook these things, we don't put them on our daily cards. The cards are used to allow us to refocus our attention on important results. It's okay to still maintain a regular to-do list of tasks that should be done, but don't affect your yearlong or ultimate goals. Many people like to write everything down.

Having a card of daily priority tasks will allow you to divert your attention periodically or deal with the inevitable distractions, and still accomplish what matters most.

## The Results for Attention

The 3x5 card experiment might help you realize that you can be far more productive in controlling interruptions and distractions in order to focus attention on the task at hand. The results of our observations helped us understand several important things.

First, we realized stopping interruptions and focusing on the most important tasks required a strategy for our work. Tactics work best when serving a deliberate strategy—otherwise, chaos reigns.

Without a clear focus, we found that, rather than working a deliberate strategy, we were at the mercy of not controlling distractions, not keeping a schedule, and not saying no to new projects that would throw us off track from the important work to be done.

We realized that saying "no" was particularly important. Because we each had a limited amount of time and resources available, we sometimes needed to make it clear—including to the "boss," when needed—that in order to take on another task, we would need to adjust the schedule to allow for it.

Saying "yes" to a new task meant something else would not be done or would take longer to complete. It's the boss's responsibility to make a call on which thing should take priority.

Next, we needed to better control interruptions. Some of the things we did included closing our email programs and checking mail only at preplanned times that served our individual schedules (for me, 11:30 a.m. and 3:30 p.m. most days). You can do this in your own life. Most things that arrive by email can wait one to three hours for your attention.

After getting the approval of supervisors, some of us started closing office doors and putting a sticky note on the door saying we would be available at a certain time. This helped control drop-ins and the distraction of people just walking by the door.

Some of us even put our phones on do not disturb during the time we wanted to focus. It's easy to establish a system so that the most vital calls—like emergency calls from family members—can still get through.

Our primary effort was to carve out a block or two of uninterrupted time each day during which we could put forth a concentrated effort focusing on our most important task on the list.

If you want to be truly productive, and move toward your goals, you must make available true, uninterrupted time in which you can focus. Here are a few additional strategies we found useful:

- Block out time on your calendar to focus on tasks. Many of us share our calendars, so anyone with access to yours will see the blocked-out time.
- Let people know ahead of time that you need a portion of your day to put your undivided attention into whatever it is.
- Make an agreement in the office that, for the sake of personal productivity, it is acceptable to close and place a do not disturb (DND) sign on the office door for periods in which you need uninterrupted time. Be sure to take a break every

hour or so to stay fresh, yet continue to watch out for distractions.

- Put a temporary away or unavailable message on your phone and email.
- Go to a different location. For most of my writing projects, I often take my laptop to the library, a park, or a coffee shop.
- Don't know where your time is getting away from you? Start a log of interruptions, to gain an understanding of who, what, when, where, and how they happen.
- Improve your ability to say no by practicing it whenever it makes sense. When someone drops by asking you to join them on a break, if it's not time for your break yet, just say no, thank you. If someone tries to engage you in anything off-topic, let them know you're busy.
- Set limits. When someone stops in and just wants to talk, tell them you have two minutes or so, or ask them to come back at a designated break time.

What other ideas can you add that would work for you? How you manage distractions and interruptions will depend on the kind of work you do and the kind of company you work for. You can find more ideas online about stopping or limiting interruptions in different kinds of workplaces.

We've been talking about managing your time so you have time to take action. You'll need to take action on these ideas, too!

Seeing interruptions for what they are and thinking about them differently might allow you to take actions you would not have considered. Giving yourself the gift of precious time will go a long way in making it possible to reap a new result.

Take action on some of the ideas to limit interruptions and better structure your time now. You won't regret it.

To inspire you, here's one of my old daily 3x5 card lists from when I worked in a large, multi-national company:

- Memo to sales managers for major projects list
- Review financials for Western region
- Complete executive summary for monthly report
- Select location for quarterly strategy meeting
- Review and comment on new collateral materials

This was a typical, if somewhat long list. In reality, there were days when I would not complete a single task on such a list because ... well, you know, *things happen*. This particular list took me two long days to complete. Yet, knowing what I know now, if I had put in a concerted, uninterrupted effort, I could have easily scratched off every item on this list in a few hours.

If you have a complicated job or a complex life, you might need to keep a master task list of long-range projects and choose two to five to add to your daily index card. Not every task comes with a deadline, so you might need to create a deadline for yourself to keep it from getting bypassed day after day.

It takes a serious and conscious effort to make the best use of your time. It's a skill that gets better with practice, and it's worth the effort. Just imagine how much more you can accomplish if you focus your energy for chunks of time.

All of this boils down to one simple realization: If we do not plan our work and work our plan, we are at the mercy of countless things that will derail us. Life is full of random opportunities for distraction.

Your strategy does not have to be elaborate by any means. It just needs to provide an outcome and some guardrails to keep you on track. I wrote out my strategy as a sort of mission statement for time management:

"To remain conscious of and control my time by controlling distractions to become as productive as possible while reducing stress. At the end of each month I will review my progress and make the necessary adjustments to further enhance my efficiency (doing things right) and effectiveness (doing the right things)."

This simple strategy pointed me in the direction of being productive, while also helping me find ways to reduce enormous amounts of stress that my lack of a plan had created.

By the way, you'll notice I use Peter Drucker's definition: "Efficiency is doing things right, effectiveness is doing the right things." If you want to be both efficient and effective, you'll need to keep this definition in mind!

Your boss will notice your efforts at time management—and if they don't, an added benefit of using 3x5 cards each day is that they provide a complete list of the most important work you have accomplished. Imagine bringing that list to your next personnel review. How many people can do that?

The crux of this section is simply this: Be thoughtful and deliberate about where you place your effort and spend your time. Learn from others, explore, and choose the ideas and methods that resonate with you most.

## Giving Voice to Your Choice

Once you fine-tune your ability to see what is important in a given day, with a maximum of two to five items on your list, you are positioned to make better choices.

By limiting the list to the most important items with the questions we asked above—*What will the impact of this be a year from now?* and *How does this task fit with my purpose and vision in life?*—we were able to be more productive during the day than we had ever been. Even taking on the lowest-ranked item of the five produced far better results than our former method of "winging it."

However, we would always try to focus first on the item that was most important to us, and then the next, and so on. As we experimented and learned the system, our choices became easy and natural.

Imagine choosing to do something each day from your thoughtful list of a few things that will make the most impact in your life a year from now. This is very powerful indeed.

Here's a little rhyme I started using many years ago, as I saw it play out in my life many times:

*Mile by mile* can be a trial,
*Yard by yard* can still be hard,
But *inch by inch*, anything's a cinch!

Imagine the effect of accumulating just one thing each workday. That's 250 (five days x fifty weeks) meaningful, completed tasks during a year.

When you position yourself to accomplish a little each day, the cumulative effect is truly life changing. Just think, if you even achieved *half* of that—125 meaningful things in a year—it would be far more than the average person dares to attempt. That rate would put you at the top of the performance curve.

If you work in a company that conducts performance reviews, think what keeping track of these accomplishments will do when you sit down with your boss at review time!

How many people take the time to write down their accomplishments? I can tell you from experience, it is not very many. Yet the benefit is so great now that you know it, how can you pass up on doing it?

As Ken Blanchard once said, "There's a difference between interest and commitment. When you're *interested* in doing something, you do it only when it's convenient. When you're committed to something, you accept no excuses, only results." Choose to commit, not quit!

Unless you commit to the choice you've made and see it through, what chance is there it would have been accomplished? Not much. But when you can see the choice as important to your future, you will make a firm commitment to it, and then you will act on it. How can you fail?

The likelihood of your success increases significantly when you are committed to making it happen. Be intentional in your choices, and they will serve you well. I can't emphasize strongly enough how important it is to commit! This is your life. If you can't commit to success in your life, why are you here?

Now that you've made your primary choice and committed to it for the day, you're able to do something about it. In other words, you are in a position to begin acting on it by applying *effort*.

## Effortless Effort

Many good habits, over time, become effortless. They also effortlessly lead you into other habits. When you invest in the list-making effort, for example, other small but effective efforts often follow.

Want to know an interesting thing about the efforts we make each day? They're generally divided. Divided how? Think about a typical day at work. Sometimes we are able to focus on one thing, putting all of our time, energy, and attention into it. What happens? We see results and either complete the task at hand or make good progress on it. Yet with the pressures and distractions so common in life and at work, how often does that really happen?

The reality for most of us is, we wind up attempting to work on *more than* one thing, even though some of these things do little or nothing to create the future we want!

Why do we do this? It seems to be the generally accepted way that people do things, doesn't it? Society praises multitaskers, when the reality is that doing multiple things at the same time is a terrible way to achieve results.

Why don't we know this? Because when we're multitasking, we can't see the forest for the trees!

Is it any wonder so many accomplish so little, and a few can accomplish so much? When you place your attention on doing the right things, you not only reap what you really want, but you also reduce the clutter of unproductive activities and the frustration of working hard and seeming to get nowhere. You transition to getting more of what you really want, and less of what you don't want!

To become responsible for your efforts is to become disciplined and mature. Without consistent, meaningful work, life is far less fulfilling. With a disciplined lifestyle, we contribute more to our families and friends. Remember, your life exists in relationships, and relationships thrive when you have dedicated time to them.

The theme of this chapter captures everything you need to fulfill your destiny: Take action, and you will reap the rewards over and over again throughout your life!

In case you didn't notice, we once again see the S.T.A.R. pattern in ACE:

- Attention = See
- Choice = Think
- Effort = Act

Then Reap the rewards!

I'll end this section with a little analogy. In our yard we have many squirrels. They keep busy much of the year building nests, mating, chasing each other, and gathering acorns.

One thing I admire about these furry little creatures is their diligence. They always seem to be doing something worthwhile, whether it's making a place to live, propagating, having fun, or saving for the future. That's pretty much our existence too, isn't it?

In this book, we are focusing on how to make life meaningful and worthwhile. Be like the squirrel—enjoy your life and gather plenty of acorns along the way! We will discuss what you can do with the extra acorns later in this book.

I would be remiss if I didn't include one last thing here. Think about who can help you build accountability for the process. Find a colleague, boss, friend, acquaintance, or spouse with whom you can openly discuss each week how you are doing with ACE.

Sharing your plan with someone else will help you sharpen the skills so it becomes natural to you. In asking for accountability, the success you enjoy will be, without a doubt, considerable.

In Chapter 7 we will expand further on taking action.

## CHAPTER SUMMARY

- Consider where and how you spend your time.
- ACE it! — Attention, Choice, Effort.
- You can realistically get very few major things done each day, so choose to do those that are *most important* to building your future.
- Increase your personal productivity by controlling interruptions. Don't try to multitask!
- The cumulative effect of individual accomplishments over time can be considerable.
- Consider the life of a squirrel. Be busy, but purposeful.

**Questions and activities to deepen my learning from this chapter:**

- What do I choose to commit to take action on today? Tomorrow? For the week?
- What steps can I take to control interruptions?
- What time-wasting activities can I say NO to?
- Mark time on my calendar for uninterrupted work.
- I will consider using the 3x5 card method or an electronic version of it.
- What other method(s) can I use to remind me of what's important and to record individual accomplishments for future reflection?

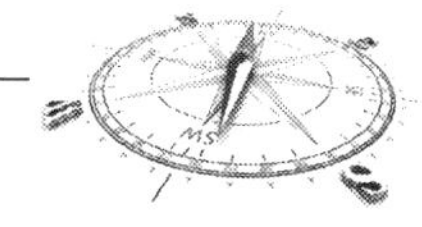

CHAPTER 4

# — REAP —
# Reaping the Rewards

*"Sow a thought, and you reap an act;*
*Sow an act, and you reap a habit;*
*Sow a habit and you reap a character;*
*Sow a character, and you reap a destiny."*
—Charles Reade

In this last chapter of Section 1, let's pull everything together and tie it up with a bright red ribbon.

As mentioned previously, each part of the S.T.A.R. Approach builds on the last and does not stand alone. In other words, *seeing* new things creates new *thoughts,* motivating new *actions,* resulting in *reaping* something new. Or put another way, the more you see and the clearer it is, the greater your ability to think in new ways and reflect in a way that deepens your understanding. With these new thoughts and deeper understanding, you're able to make better decisions and choose what to do, leading to new and well-defined actions.

Thinking in this new way can produce life-shaping results, on which you can continue to build. Out of this cycle come the benefits of a life that is fuller and lived with more intention, that is less driven by your emotions and the pressure of others.

Instead of reacting or responding to circumstances, you sit in the driver's seat, so you might literally reach a new destination, far beyond anywhere you dreamed possible.

In our last diagram we used a target to explain how each part of the process is incorporated into the next. This allows us to see it all starts at the center. It shows us that, without *seeing* first, the remainder doesn't happen. There is one more thing to add to this graphic. Notice the arrow going from Reap to See.

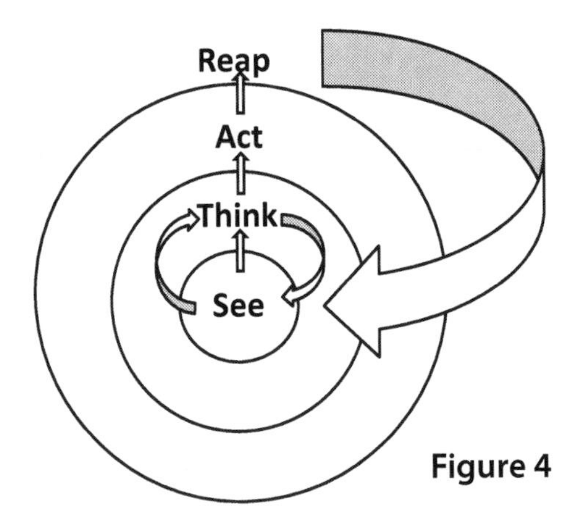


Figure 4

As we enhance our ability to see more, we broaden our thinking, which leads us to take new actions and reap more results. Then what happens? In going through this process, we find *the more we reap, the more we see*. Another feature of S.T.A.R. is that each iteration is a cycle that builds on itself.

## Following the Cycle

The reason we pay attention to a cycle, or pattern, is that it allows us to continually create new results in our lives. Understanding this can help us produce something meaningful, something of significance. By following such a process, you are literally building and strengthening the foundation on which your life is built.

Each time you go through a cycle, you position yourself to better see and think about what action you will take next. Isn't that what experience is all about?

For example, as you gain more experience at work, you create the ability to see more opportunities. Most people advance in their careers by building on results over time. Because the S.T.A.R. process is cyclical, each iteration has the potential to allow you to see more clearly and find more opportunity. With each cycle, you experience new and better results.

Have you ever considered how you can build on reaping the fruits of your labor? Perhaps you've heard the old saying, "What you appreciate, appreciates"? In other words, what you appreciate increases in value. Reaping is NOT the end of the cycle; it's a doorway into the first phase of the next cycle.

By appreciating and looking closely at what you reaped, you can be better informed to **see** more, on which you become more thoughtful in your **think**ing, upon which you can make better choices on which to take **act**ion, leading you to a place in which you **reap** more, from which you can continue the cycle.

Isn't life like that—full of cycles? There are cycles throughout history of feast and famine, peace and war, life and death. There is the cycle of the earth's travel around the sun, from which we receive our seasons, which continue to cycle year after year, adding to the richness of life. The entire universe is filled with cycles.

For our purposes, the definition of *cycle* is "a series of events that are regularly repeated in the same order." You can think of a cycle as a pattern that can be seen or noticed. While there are many permutations a cycle can take, let's look at three types as they relate to S.T.A.R.

## The 'Vicious' Cycle

We'll start with what's called a *vicious cycle,* because this cycle is well known in the modern world. The perfect example is addiction.

Addictions to things like drugs, alcohol, or cigarettes are all too common, so we know how these cycles work. Addictions tend to feed themselves—each time the craving is indulged, it leads to more craving. Addiction can become a continuous downward spiral that ultimately ends in misery or death.

Like most vicious cycles, addictions often start small and grow more destructive with repetition. In a vicious cycle, the results reinforce themselves, but to your detriment.

A vicious cycle does not have to be a major addiction, however. It may start as something as simple as a bad attitude. A bad attitude about your work or spouse, for example, can lead to you complaining, which feels momentarily satisfying. But complaint draws more negative energy, and creates more to complain about. A bad attitude addiction can ultimately destroy your career or marriage.

When you look for patterns in your life, be sure to check for vicious cycles and figure out where you can break the cycle, before it hurts you.

## The Closed-Ended Loop

Next is a closed-ended or standalone loop, repeated one at a time, each loop independent of the next. In other words, each loop stands on its own, with little or no influence from one loop to the next. Think of it as:

See – think – act – reap. Completed.

When we do not learn or build on the results of a cycle, we tend to achieve a closed end where we receive something once but do not build on it. Television can be like this. We can sit and watch television for pure entertainment day after day, year after year—yet when we walk away from the TV, we are no different than when we sat down. We have learned nothing.

If every time you pay your annual income taxes, you wish you'd paid more attention to saving receipts; and if every time you step on the scale, you wish you'd said no to a few more desserts; but you never actually MAKE these changes—you may be in a Closed-Ended Loop.

## The Virtuous Cycle

The third type of cycle has the potential for spiraling upward, ever-expanding with each cycle feeding into the next cycle so that at least a part of the benefit of the previous cycle makes the next cycle better or larger.

The virtuous cycle, which I often refer to as the creating cycle, literally builds on itself, expanding and creating more and more over time. Such things as a growing business or a healthy workout program can be described this way.

To change a do-nothing closed-ended cycle into a virtuous cycle only requires that we examine the cycle more closely, learn, and grow from it.

If you want to improve your business or your relationship with your wife, examine what you are doing and see the patterns in the cycles. If you find a good pattern, build on it. Often, we notice what we should have done just at the moment when it's too late. Get ahead of that pattern and make changes now.

And if you notice a vicious cycle, stop it immediately—not "next time"!

As I've pointed out a number of times, there is nothing more important in life than our relationships. Life *is* relationship. Let's look at one key relationship: marriage.

You'll find many cycles that exist in a marriage, so let's choose one, such as spending time together. When we can see the value of our time together, reflect on what it means, and take actions to enhance it, we will reap true rewards!

Isn't this how most romantic relationships begin? You see this lovely person, and all you can think about is her. You take actions to do things for her, and ultimately win her hand in marriage.

For a time, this is such a virtuous cycle. Then, because we see the person so much, we begin taking them for granted and stop the thoughts we had and the actions that made it so great. Neglect sets in.

What's the result of this neglect? We stop appreciating and reaping. Thus begins the closed-ended loop. This cycle can repeat, sometimes for years, with nothing new or exciting ever happening. Many times, close-ended cycles evolve into vicious, downward cycles where bickering or feeling victimized feed each person temporary relief. The ending is divorce for many couples. But you can see how stopping the close-ended cycle before it turned vicious could have turned the marriage around!

Apply this concept of a vicious or virtuous cycle to your business, your job, or any of your relationships and you will see the same pattern. All it takes for the vicious cycle to begin is to stop *appreciating* what we have. So, for us to truly capitalize on the creating cycle foundation in the S.T.A.R. Approach, we must realize that appreciating is part of reaping. If you like what you have created, you have to be *grateful* for it. That way, you'll see it, consider it, act on it, and continue the virtuous cycle of life and receiving more.

Figure 5 is a visual of a virtuous cycle, starting at the bottom, where you begin with seeing a new thing, deliberating on it, acting, and reaping a result, thus gaining the ability to see more as you go through the cycle. On this you again think, act, and reap, building on the previous cycle.

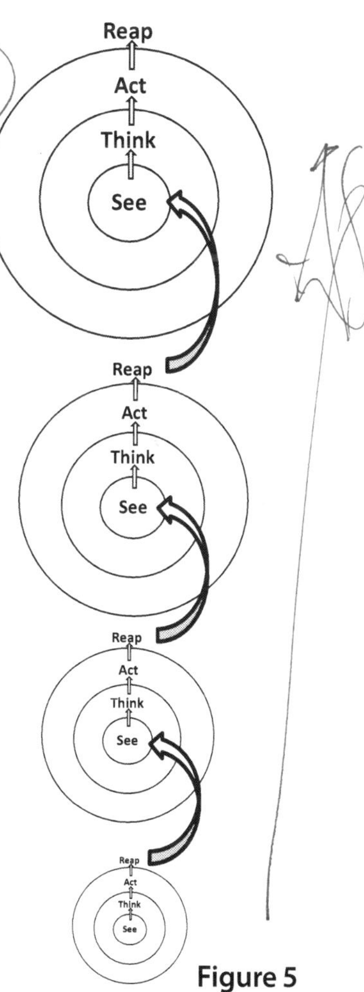

Figure 5

Each successive loop builds on the preceding loop. How long can this go on? Well, look at your life. Isn't this similar to how we grow as we build ourselves, our lives, and pretty much everything else? It only stops when *we* stop, at the end of this physical life.

Life is full of each of these types of cycles. The thing to notice, however, is that by building on a cycle, you can enhance the next cycle and beyond. That's why it is important to "see" and understand how you are reaping your results. When you learn from something and incorporate what you have learned into the next cycle and continue to build—wow! The results can become greater and greater, far exceeding anything you ever thought you could reap.

An example of this shows up in many people's careers. We may start at a lower position and, over time, progress to a more responsible position, from which we often move to an even greater position. "Climbing the corporate ladder" is a prime example of a virtuous cycle.

But if we were to continue doing exactly what we did at the onset of our career—never evolving and merely reaping what we did from the outset, without incorporating what we have learned—we would wind up stuck and never advance.

Let's face it—the reality is this happens to most of us at some point in our careers.

Yet when we *do* continue to learn and grow, we often progress from one position to the next, or we learn how to expand the position itself, or we make a lateral move into something even more rewarding and more in alignment with our long-term goals.

With each positive change in a career comes some kind of benefit. Such benefits can include greater earnings and other financial rewards, more respect and prestige in our business and industry, a corner office, or many other things.

Stop and notice what you have earned at this point in your life. *Appreciate* it. Take all the lessons you can from how you have developed. Continue to create something new, and keep growing into the future. That's how you can cycle through life with ever-increasing positive results.

Look for some of the more important cycles in your life. As you do this, and you begin to "see" more, you can begin to build your life on purpose, with intention.

To start the process, stop and consider what you have gained from some actions you have taken in your life, whether in your career, your marriage, or your personal or professional life. Stop now and find at least one thing. What do you notice? What does the current result tell you? If the result you have received is not exactly what you want, what can you learn from that information?

Find the lesson from whatever has happened and go after what you DO want! Can it be that simple? Yes it can, and we will dig deeper into the topic of reaping in Chapter 8.

To uncover more patterns in your life, complete **Exercise 2 in Section 3** entitled "Cycles/Patterns."

## Sowing Seeds and Reaping

We've mentioned the analogy of sowing seeds and working your fields to produce a positive result—and how neglecting your field or garden will inevitably produce a weedy, rocky mess.

Now let's give some thought to what you are producing. Are you sowing the *right* seeds? Are you sowing *enough* seeds?

Because life doesn't exist without relationships, this seems like a good place to sow, doesn't it? If you are sowing in your relationships—making time to stay in touch with and care about the people you love—you will certainly reap more from life.

How about your spiritual life? What seeds are you sowing there? If you sow the right seeds, through meditation or contemplation and study and prayer, there will certainly be a harvest of peace and satisfaction.

Are you sowing seeds of growth and leadership into yourself? Are you studying great leaders, making contacts with people you admire, networking within your field? If so, you will surely reap a harvest that could be great for your life and for others.

Give some time to thinking on what you've planted and how it will provide a harvest. Whether you choose to sow or not, you will reap some kind of harvest. Sowing seeds or good deeds and hard work will grow you a bountiful crop, while failing to plant seed—well, I think you understand that you'll get the limited value of a plot of weeds.

It's always your choice. It's your future. If you do the right thing now, you can reap the right thing later.

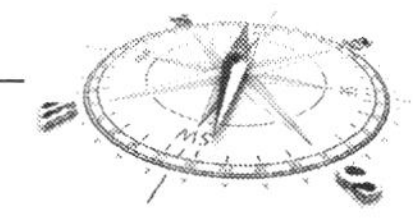

# Section 1 Conclusion

Before moving on to Section 2 of this book, let's discuss the type of life you wish to build. You can do this by adding one last thing to See, Think, Act, Reap … another S.

This S is the culmination of your results. It is what you are driving toward and is a summation of the results of your life.

It's not **Success**. Although you will be more successful.

It's not **Seeing** more. Yet you will certainly see more.

It's not **Satisfaction**. But you will be more satisfied.

It's not **Smiling**. But you will smile far more often.

You can build a life that is all about yourself. You can build a life that is all about others. While success can be defined in many ways, building **significance** is less about you and more about others.

## Success vs. Significance

Success is typically inward focused, working *in* your life. When you are no longer alive, your personal success ends—at least, we know that on the earth, it ends.

Significance is focused outward and is about working on your life and helping others. When you are no longer alive, the result of what you did can continue to make an impact. How? Through those you lived for and those whose lives you contributed to. Your results live on through others.

What will you leave behind? In the end, will others benefit from the life you lived?

You can write books and leave your life experiences and the wisdom gained for others to learn and grow from and change in their lives. You can leave what's left of your money as an inheritance to your family members, but you know it will likely be quickly consumed and short-lived. It might be better to leave money in a private foundation or trust that pays out its earnings in perpetuity to charities you care about.

Your memory itself can be a legacy, if you tried to live your life as a good example. By the example you became, you can leave a legacy in your children, your family, and others, one that will go from their lives into others' lives, including their children's children and beyond.

When you think about a person whose significance carries on, although they might be long dead, who comes to mind? For me, it's people in the history of our great country, such as George Washington, Abraham Lincoln, Thomas Jefferson, John Adams, and many other major figures.

In the business world, it is those that have made an impact on my life in some way, such as Andrew Carnegie, Henry Ford, Thomas Watson Jr., Steve Jobs, and many others.

Then there are the people who influenced millions with their words, whether spoken or in books. People like Paul of Tarsus, Saint

Augustine, C. S. Lewis, Ed Cole, and others who wrote books that were especially meaningful to me—Jim Rohn, Robert Fritz, John Maxwell, Michael Gerber, and many, many others.

Last, but certainly not least, are those who influenced my personal life, such as two of my old bosses, Alan Durant and Bill Brown; two of my pastors, Nathan Ridgeway and Aubrey Shines; and my wife Jane and Aunt Alice. All of these people have made a lasting impact on my life and are a significant factor in the legacy I create.

At the end of life, it's not the success you've enjoyed, or the fact that you saw more than others, or that you smiled more and were happy that matters. What is far more important is what resulted from the things you said and did.

It will be important that your life had meaning, and purpose, and that you impacted others. In other words, you led a life of *significance*.

I believe that, deep in each of our hearts, almost everyone wants the same thing—to leave their footprint on this earth. We all want to affect other people's lives in a positive way, and to leave a legacy that lives on, continuing to make its mark long after we're gone.

You might say, but I'm not Thomas Jefferson or Andrew Carnegie! How can my simple life be significant to the world?

Let's realize a truth about life. Some time ago, I heard it said that "all change happens in relationship." So far, I have found zero exceptions to this statement.

This book is about *change*. Change for good. Change for creating a new and different life. And as we've already emphasized, life and relationship are synonymous.

This book is about intentionally creating our lives to better the world around us. This book is about finding ways to help us live a more fulfilling life, becoming more of who we are capable of becoming, and touching others in a way that lives beyond us.

Face it: One day, you and I will no longer be here. What would you like to be said about you after you're gone? "Who was he? Never heard of him." Or would you rather that it is said: "Yes, she/he affected other people's lives in a good way. Their life truly mattered. I would like to become like him/her. She/he lived a life that made a difference."

If you take nothing else away from the book, I hope you will decide to do this: work on you and work on your life. Don't just continue working *in* it. Your life is who you are and what comes out of your being. That's what determines the course of your life.

Always work on who you are becoming. Don't just make quick and simple choices in life. Instead, use the gifts you've been given to be more thoughtful, and then do something. Act on your choices in a creative way.

Begin now. Find a way. Turn your life into one of significance. Develop a vision of what you want the outcome of your life to be. You have the ability in you to create practically anything you want!

I challenge you to become all you can be. Become more for your family and friends. Live a life of significance and be fulfilled, leaving a legacy behind of the exceptional human being you are and grew to become. Start now!

# SECTION 2

# Digging Deeper

# Overview

In this section we are going to dig deeper into seeing, thinking, acting, and reaping, to discover how it personally relates to you, your life, and your future.

At the end of the section, we will take a look at the S.T.A.R. Approach as a whole. Something to consider as you work through the content is that you can create practically anything you want when you see it clearly, consider it thoughtfully, and take the right actions.

Most live life in what Robert Fritz calls a "reactive/responsive" orientation. What does this look like? People most often react or respond in a way that does not create, but rather traps them in a problem-solving mode of trying to fix a problem. As a result of this stagnancy, life continues to move them back and forth in an oscillating pattern with no real progress.

Most people become subject to their circumstances and environment rather than taking control of them. An example is in the chronic dieting many people experience. They lose some weight, which lets the pressure off a little, and then they gain it back, which puts the pressure on them to lose weight again. They continue to lose and gain, and lose and gain, and often wind up worse off than at the beginning. You might recognize this pattern from Chapter 4: the vicious cycle. The underlying reason for all of this? Fritz would say it's faulty structure.

What Fritz suggests is that, rather than just trying to solve each problem as it arises, you create what you want. Become intentional and deliberate about seeing the outcome you want to construct.

How can we get into this proactive mindset? First, develop an acquired taste for seeing your current reality, which will help to ground you in what is *real* instead of a *fantasy*.

Once you have your footing and sights set on your goals, you can cultivate a healthy tension that eliminates the old responsive/reactive, oscillating pattern. With a new awareness and approach, you can far more easily create the outcomes you want in your personal and professional life.

Another way of saying this is that, when you are in the reactive/responsive orientation, you are subject to it. If you can't see it or don't realize it's there, you will be blindly controlled by it.

Think of how a river flows down a riverbed. The water follows the riverbed contained within its banks and will continue doing so unless the riverbed is changed. The course of the river *can* be changed by altering its path—through damming and re-digging a new route. The Army Corps of Engineers has done this many times!

In this analogy, the water is the flow of your life, and the riverbed is the underlying structure that you naturally follow, hardly realizing it's there. Your life will flow within the banks of this underlying structure (path) forever.

For the most part, you are blind to the underlying structure that is in control. But in the creative orientation, you not only see the underlying structure, but you take steps to change it.

I highly recommend picking up a copy of Robert Fritz's book *The Path of Least Resistance* to help you more fully understand where you are in relation to the path toward creating.

The following pages and the tools in the Section 3 provide a more in-depth way to create more of what you want in life.

Always remember: This is your life. You may, of course, choose to do as you wish. One choice is to follow the status quo, but you know that can lead to stagnation. Another choice is to learn and grow and evolve.

If you are deliberate in your choice, you can create the future you truly want.

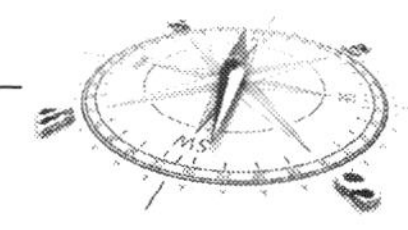

# CHAPTER 5

# Seeing in New Ways

## What Time Is It Anyway?

Time, your most precious resource, is also your most limited. Sure, it may seem like you have many years ahead of you, and I hope you do—yet what if you don't? Before you know it, tomorrow is here. I've already lived more than two-thirds of my life, provided I make it to one hundred! Time certainly does fly, and it seems to go faster the older you get.

In reality, no one is promised tomorrow, but one can hope. Want to make the most of your time? It is beneficial to routinely stop and reflect on this most precious resource and the life you have.

Ask yourself this question: "What am I doing with my time?" (Hint: This is synonymous with "What am I doing with my life?")

So, what *are* you doing with your time and life? Literally, how are you *spending* it?

With a seeming abundance of time, especially when we're young, most of us give time little or no thought. Yet what we *do* with our time now determines much of what *happens* in our future. What we do with our time sets us up for success or failure, significance or insignificance. By simply seeing time as valuable, our perspective shifts from that of its obscurity to that of its relevance. How often are you aware of time? It's a good question to ponder.

There's a funny thing about our discussion of time. It might seem like a waste to slow down, to stop and consider time. I get the irony, but it is in this slowing down and thinking that we actually enhance our use of time. When we are always rushing through life, how much of what we do can be genuinely thoughtful and deliberate?

We literally must pause and slow down in order to speed up the process of getting results. To go slow and see what is happening will move you to what you want more quickly. I highly recommend Kevin Cashman's book *The Pause Principle,* as it details how to slow down, step back, and take time to make great leaps forward.

*"What sleep is to the mind and body,*
*pause is to leadership and innovation."*
— Kevin Cashman

There is a cost, a price to pay, for not valuing our time. Like anything in life, what we value most will be where we place our attention and effort. If we have not really considered what we value, and what is important to us, we won't be able to see these things clearly. Without clear vision, we will stumble around, and we're likely to wind up with little more than regret.

Have you heard of the 1 in 60 rule? It's used in aviation and is based on the logic that for every one degree you travel off course for sixty miles, you will land one mile from where you had intended. If you are traveling 6,000 miles, one degree off course will land you one hundred miles from your destination. If you are traveling from the earth to the moon, one degree off course would make you miss your target by more than 4,000 miles! All that error would come from a seemingly minor, one-degree variation.

Think about this: What if you are ten degrees off course—or, heaven forbid, twenty or more degrees off—in your life? Where can you expect to land, and how far will it be from where you want to go?

The reality is that most of us are at least a few degrees off course. So how do we deal with this? Let's take a cue from aviation. When you are flying from New York to Los Angeles, numerous course corrections are required. In fact, most of the time during the flight, you are slightly off course.

Regular course corrections help you to arrive at your intended destination. Isn't life much like that? While we try our best, we drift off course frequently. It's only when we slow down and make the time to check our bearings that we can make the necessary corrections to get back on course.

The best way to accomplish this is through regular checking and adjusting. Of course, all of this depends on whether or not you know where you're going!

So, *where are you going?*

Once you know your destination, you can do what's needed to gauge and amend your course. If you do *not* have a clear understanding of where you intend to eventually be, how in the world can you get there?

This is why it is so important to begin somewhere, anywhere, with a destination in mind. Until you see and acknowledge that you know what the destination is that you desire, you are completely at the mercy of others and circumstances.

Why take the risk? My question to you is this: Where are you going? What is your destination? If you don't know, stop and think about it now. Otherwise, you might drift endlessly, winding up who knows where.

## What About the Long View?

To see more clearly in the present, it's helpful to peek into the future. By taking a long-term look at what we want, we can better see what is needed in the near-term. Like the old saying goes, "If you don't know where you're going, any road will get you there."

Don't be one of the many people who live life that way. Take your time and destination into your own hands and out of the hands of other people's intentions and unpredictable circumstances.

Let's tackle something substantial and look at what it takes to get there—the task of building a house. I've read it takes 10,000 total hours of labor to build an average-size home. Ten thousand hours is a considerable amount of time, equaling more than 400 consecutive twenty-four-hour days, or nearly five years working eight-hour days, five days a week.

Even if you have the money you need to purchase all the materials, to tackle such a task alone would be truly overwhelming for the average person.

Yet homes are built routinely. It just takes the right planning and resources, and the right team. While you *can* build one yourself, the vast majority of homes are built by a team of people. Either way will get the job done, eventually.

When faced with such a large task, the best approach is to break it down into smaller pieces and to put forth consistent effort, realizing that other people are fully involved in your life and are absolutely necessary if you are to accomplish much.

To use this basic principle: Look at the big picture and organize home-building into manageable pieces. Then look at the parts and think about which ones to tackle first and who will be involved with each piece.

Now imagine doing this with your life. All you have to do is determine what you want it to look like, plan a little, and then start building!

You've heard the old adage, "How do you eat an elephant? One bite at a time." It would take one person a long time, but one hundred people could do it far more quickly. Isn't this true for many things in life?

Are you thinking about sending your children to college and the associated costs? Managing tuition expenses can be an elephant. What we do in growing and managing our career can be an elephant. Thinking about retirement, which can be a long way off for some, can be an elephant.

Who we want to eventually become also can be an elephant. Yet, if we don't take the time to consider things of such importance, what will result?

Here's the underlying fundamental: Tackle the elephants one bite at a time. Small steps taken daily in the direction you want to go eventually create what you need, while small errors in judgment made daily compound into failure. Another way of saying it is:

> *"Failure is simply a few errors in judgment, repeated every day."*
>
> — Jim Rohn

The difference in the direction is simply tied to identifying what you really need, seeing the possibilities to fulfill that need, making the choices that align with that need, and consistently moving in that direction.

I know, I know. It's simple to say and difficult to do. But it's possible, and the choice is up to you. You can do it if you want to—or not. You can work on it and take control of your life and future—or not. To quote another famous person:

*"Whether you think you can,*
*or you think you can't—you're right."*
— Henry Ford

## The Value of Values

*"Your beliefs become your thoughts,*
*Your thoughts become your words,*
*Your words become your actions,*
*Your actions become your habits,*
*Your habits become your values,*
*Your values become your destiny."*
— Gandhi

Have you ever considered your values? For our purposes, let's define *values* as your "principles or standards of behavior; your judgment of what is important in life."

Your values significantly influence how you see the world as well as what you do and don't do. Values control which decisions you make or don't make.

When something or someone conflicts with a value you hold strongly, it can create enormous stress inside you. In other words, your values can drive your behaviors, and therefore, at least in part, contribute to your actions and the outcomes or results you obtain in life.

The better you understand what is important to you, and the influence of your values, the greater will be the opportunity to live true to yourself, with more authenticity.

Let's pause for a few minutes and do a quick check on your values in **Exercise 3 — Personal Values in Section 3**. The list will help you better define what you value. Once you've completed a fundamental appraisal of your values, you'll be able to better understand yourself.

There are no right or wrong answers. Just choose those values that seem most true to who you believe you are inside, and don't consider what you think someone else might say.

Give yourself some time to think about the top five that most resonated with you. The purpose of this exercise is to see into yourself, into who you are and what drives you and your priorities. Completing the exercise will help you better understand your needs.

To get the most out of the exercise, be sure to answer each of the questions at the end. Give some thought to each, as the answers can considerably open your mind about who you really are at this time and what you seek most in life.

## Do You Want It, or Need It?

To better see ourselves, let's start with the big picture and ask a basic question: *What is really important?*

You value many things in your life—your job, your home, your family, your friends, your car, your hobbies, and so much more.

Where does the desire for the things we value come from? Are these things truly important to us, and why?

Lying beneath the things we value are deep needs. Finding these deeper needs that drive our desires and behavior requires exploration. We need to unearth our needs so we can see them.

The best way to explore is to find the right question or questions to ask. Before developing the questions that will help you see your own life more clearly, let's discuss the difference between a *want* and a *need,* to eliminate any confusion between the two.

For our purposes *want* and *desire* are synonymous. We want many things in our lives, like a new home, a new car, a vacation, or our favorite food or flavor of ice cream. Yet we can most often do without these things or scale back with little consequence. Things we want are just that—desires we can delay or do without.

A ***want*** is something you desire but can do without. Wants are things that are nice to have, yet they're optional. A want, when fulfilled, can provide short-term satisfaction.

A ***need*** on the other hand, is far different than a want. A need is something that is *required* in life. Air, water, food, and shelter are needs. Without them, we cannot function, much less stay alive for very long. When needs are not met, life becomes a struggle. A need met leads to long-term fulfillment.

Beyond these essential needs, have you considered what you really need in life to thrive? All of us also have deep needs that, when not met, can create considerable discomfort and distress in our lives. You might need a job to earn money so you can provide for your family. You might need relationships, such as a good marriage and good friendships, to add joy to your life.

What do we need to live a life of true significance and to have lasting fulfillment? I suggest you dig in to Abraham Maslow's "Hierarchy of Needs" theory for an even deeper understanding of fundamental human need, and to gain a better understanding of yourself.

Here are some examples to help us further differentiate:

- I *need* transportation; I *want* a high-performance, expensive car.
- I *need* food to survive; I *want* ice cream.
- I *need* rest and time to recuperate; I *want* to take a long cruise to New Zealand via Hawaii.
- I *need* to work to provide for my family; I *want* to work at a high-paid, prestigious job.

These essential needs are more basic than our wants/desires. Not getting what I *want* might lead to short-term disappointment. Yet when my *needs* are unmet, the result is ongoing struggle and distress. When needs are met, the result is deep satisfaction and peace. Met needs lead to being fulfilled.

Your needs point to what's really important in your life. As we go through life, we occasionally have glimpses of our deeper needs. Most of us realize that relationships are important, for example. As the old song says, "One is the loneliest number." Yet how often do we stop and realize the true significance of relationships in our lives?

What about **time**? As we explored earlier, we each have the same amount of time in any given day. Time is our most precious and limited resource. Sure, we think about time when we are pressed on a deadline or something urgent, but what about right now? How important is your time in an ordinary day, doing ordinary things?

Since we will naturally take care of our vital needs like air, water, food, and shelter, let's not look at what we require to stay alive, but at what we need to live and thrive at the deepest levels. Our deeper needs come from within, out of what we value.

From the deep value we place on being a good provider and responsible person comes the need to support those we love by earning money to take care of our family. From the values of caring, loving, and sharing our lives comes the need for a happy relationship with our wife, child, and close friends.

These intangible needs come from who we are, from the very core of our being. These needs are what this book is really about—to become more of who you want to be, leading you toward a meaningful and fulfilling life.

One of the wisest things a person can learn in life is to understand what he really needs in life. Out of your deepest desires, or wants, arises the key to what makes you thrive. Uncovering these deep needs helps you become more aligned with who you really are and who you want to be. Once you understand what your soul needs, you can avoid the short-term, quick fixes that actually slow you down on the journey to fulfillment.

Knowing what you truly need will help you develop the strength to delay those more immediate wants or desires in order to develop wisdom and patience. This can also help you develop a greater understanding of your purpose in life and allow you to move toward it with greater ease.

What's one path to happiness? Become clear about what you value, deep inside, and then work to understand this to take a true leadership role in your life to get what you value.

Let's take a few minutes to uncover some of your deepest needs. Complete **Exercise 4 – Needs in Section 3**. This exercise will provide some valuable insight at the end of this book.

## Delayed Gratification

I'm not a fan of delayed gratification. Most people aren't, because we live in a society of instant access. With credit cards, we can buy on a whim. With fast food, we can order and eat within minutes. With online shopping, we can have virtually anything we want at the click of a button.

But is instant gratification healthy?

Delayed gratification is easy to understand, yet not so easy to do. Unless there is a deep enough understanding of what is really important to you, and a compelling reason to influence how you make decisions, it's far too easy to go for the immediate. Often this affects the long term in a significant way.

Am I saying you should put off everything in life? Of course not. We must be reasonable, and there are times when it is appropriate to indulge ourselves.

Yet having a better understanding of yourself will help with these decisions. What I'm recommending is that you carefully weigh the more important things in life, and consider the longer-term impact of your decisions. Put what is most important first instead of treating it as an afterthought.

I'll continue to enjoy my ice cream, and my hobbies, and doing many other things—but not at the expense of taking care of my deepest, long-term needs.

A good example of delayed gratification is saving for retirement. Why should someone in his twenties or thirties worry about retirement? After all, they're young and have their entire lives ahead of them. Right? So they can live for now without the end in sight or in mind. "I'll worry about the future later," they say.

Most people in my generation—the largest generation of Americans born in our country up to this point in time—will need to continue working well into their seventies and beyond. Considering the average lifespan of a male is seventy-six, it's a bit of a predicament for many—the expectation to work oneself "to death."

Yet for those who saved and consistently invested even a small part of their income, their lives will be far simpler and they'll have less worry as they age.

While Social Security was never meant to be a retirement plan, the generations after my group of "baby boomers" will likely have it in some lesser form, if at all. The spend now, worry later mindset will create even greater consequences. Knowing what is important to you can help you move to a save now, spend later mindset.

Think about the second largest investment most of us make: a car. During the course of a lifetime, you will likely purchase several cars.

If you make an average income throughout your life, you will spend many tens of thousands—perhaps hundreds of thousands—of dollars from the time you complete school until you attempt to retire in your sixties.

By simply purchasing reasonably priced cars that have lower costs to operate, and driving them longer during a forty-year period, you can save a significant amount of money for later. Wouldn't it be nice to have some of that money available to enjoy retirement, or to merely ease the worry of not having enough money as you go through life?

You can ride around in a gorgeous car, looking good doing it, satisfying the ol' ego, and wind up paying in the end—dearly. Or you can ride around in a quality car with considerable savings, enjoying more peace of mind, and have less struggle at the end of your life.

Which strategy makes more sense to you?

The same exercise can be done for your home, eating out less, and many other things. A great piece of advice a friend once gave me was: "It's what you *don't spend* that matters later." He's so right.

Cars, homes, and other such things are important—yet what about the most important thing in life, your relationships? Spending time with your wife or child every day can add up to a considerable investment over a lifetime.

Don't come to regret what was not created in your friendships when you had the chance. The value of the time you spend with others cannot be calculated.

It took me far too many years to come to this realization.

## Regret

At the age of fifty-one, I became a widower. My wife had gotten cancer and the first diagnosis gave her three to five years to live—yet it was not to be. The cancer spread quickly through her body and they shortened the outlook to eighteen months. Within six months, she passed.

To say I was devastated would be an understatement. I met Charlotte during my senior year in high school, and we were married at nineteen. For thirty-two years, we were by each other's sides, with all the successes and challenges that come with a marriage. In the end, she died a horribly painful death.

To this day, I wish I hadn't been so busy with work that I missed a lot of time with her and our daughter.

While our life together was not perfect, it was full of love and laughter, triumphs, and victories. Charlotte taught me to always look for the good in life, and her strong faith in Christ continues to be an example to me in how to live a Christian life.

believe that death is not the end—but I also know that, to fail to live our lives with purpose can bring many regrets. As Jim Rohn once said, "We must all suffer from one of two pains: the pain of discipline or the pain of regret. The difference is, discipline weighs ounces while regret weighs tons."

I am thankful for the thirty-two years I had with Charlotte and all I learned from her. Looking back, I do have some regrets, because I didn't put our relationship first at times. But overall, we had a good life together, and my regrets are few.

## A New Frame of Mind

Before wrapping up this chapter, let's discuss a fundamental that affects everything you see and think—your frame of mind or *mindset*. I'll dedicate the rest of this chapter to introducing you to two concepts can help you see yourself and your goals more accurately.

### Mindset

The first concept is that of mindset, which everyone uses in practically every situation. Want a detailed exploration of how to unearth your mindset? Check out Carol Dweck's excellent book entitled *Mindset*, which I highly recommend you add to your reading list.

To quote Dr. Dweck: "For thirty years, my research has shown that the view you adopt for yourself profoundly affects the way you lead your life."

She points out there are essentially two mindsets in everything we do in life. One is the *fixed mindset*, which creates urgency in us to prove ourselves over and over. The second, a *growth mindset*, happens when you don't place restrictions on yourself regarding your ability to learn and cultivate the qualities you want through your efforts.

We all approach almost everything in life from one of these two mindsets. To be able to recognize which mindset you are using can dramatically affect your life and the course you are on.

A fixed mindset is self-limiting, making you hold back from moving forward to something new, something that will stretch you. It is focused on what you *cannot* do and the abilities and capabilities you *don't think* you have. You will steer clear of any possible failure. The results received from this mindset will undoubtedly be fewer.

A growth mindset removes these self-induced restrictions and sets the belief that one can learn and grow almost any ability or capability. The growth mindset says that you are not stuck with what you currently have available to you. You will take on a challenge, even if it might mean failing, because you know that failing does not make you a failure. Rather, every experience can become part of learning and growth. You know you can do more and have more when you do not place limits or restrictions on yourself.

A fixed mindset *restricts*.

A growth mindset *expands*.

We have only lightly touched on the surface of this concept, but if it interests you, I recommend picking up a copy of Dr. Dweck's book.

## Noticing

Let's wrap this chapter up with a word you may have noticed throughout this book—*notice*.

When you *notice* something, you become aware and "see" the previously unnoticed or unseen. It's been there all along, but something happened, and you suddenly paid attention to it.

It might be that someone pointed something out, or you just happened to be in a state of mind to see it. If you can slow down and notice what people are saying and doing, or what is there or what is happening, it can change how you see things around you.

If you notice things that have previously gone unnoticed, things that you've been totally blind to, what will happen? You might discover a lot!

Many of us run through life in such a hurry that we pass right by the obvious. We might find ourselves working to the point of becoming a workaholic and completely ignoring our families and friends.

How many times have you driven somewhere and when you arrived you could barely remember any details about the trip? Have you ever been on the phone and passed right by the exit where you needed to get off the highway?

How many times has someone been speaking while you concentrated so much on what you planned to say or how you planned to respond that you missed part of what they were saying? In the era of cell phones, have you been guilty of being so absorbed in your phone that you don't hear or see what's happening right in front of you?

To become more aware, slow down. Pay attention and use your senses of sight, hearing, smell, touch, and taste. Become curious and look for things you've not previously seen.

The key here is to slow down so you can begin to *see more*. When you do, you will come across to others as more caring, more interested and interesting, more personable, more valued, and more respectful.

Don't the people you interact with daily deserve to be respected? Of course they do! When you take the time to notice more, you will begin to respect and value your associates and even your own life more.

I leave you with one last thought:

> *"If leaders today do not step back, to stop momentum, to gain perspective, to transcend the immediacies of life, and to accelerate their leadership, we will continue to crash economically, personally and collectively."*
>
> — Kevin Cashman

## CHAPTER SUMMARY

- Time is your most precious and limited resource. Use it well!
- To make better progress and decisions, learn to slow down and pause.
- Determining your most important values helps you see inside yourself.
- Your deepest needs can determine your life path.
- A growth mindset expands, while a fixed mindset restricts.
- What you don't notice about yourself can hold you back.
- Your beliefs ultimately become your destiny.

**Questions and activities to deepen my learning from this chapter:**

- In the long run, what am I doing with the hours I have available to me?
- Am I spending my time in ways that are aligned with what I value?
- Have I unearthed my deepest needs? Are they truly *needs*, or are they *wants*?
- What am I noticing about myself and my life?
- I will uncover my needs by completing **Exercise 4 in Section 3**.

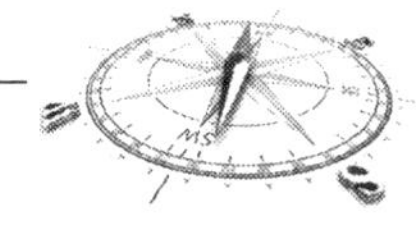

CHAPTER 6

# Thinking in New Ways

Take a look at your day so far today. What have you accomplished today? What have you spent your time doing?

If you had to account for each hour, and even each minute, how much time do you waste and how much do you use wisely? (Of course, reading this book is considered a wise use of time, if I do say so myself.)

The point is, some of the time you spent today probably passed by unnoticed. Our thoughts can slip by unnoticed as well. What do you think about throughout the day? Do you think about what is most important to you, or is your brain jumbled with random musings that have little significance?

With so many things to think about, where does one start? The answer is as individual as you are. But you *can* find a way to rein in your thoughts and use them to your advantage.

at way to begin is using a decision or priority matrix, as shown in a condensed form below. A full version is provided in **Exercise 5 of Section 3**. Before moving to it, let's discuss the matrix and its use.

**Priority Matrix**

| | **Urgent** | **Not Urgent** |
|---|---|---|
| **Important** | **Responding Quadrant**<br>**Important and Urgent**<br>**Manage**<br>Must be done out of necessity | **Creating Quadrant**<br>**Important and Not Urgent**<br>**Focus**<br>Creating your future |
| **Not Important** | **Reacting Quadrant**<br>**Not Important and Urgent**<br>**Avoid**<br>A poor use of time - deception | **Reacting Quadrant**<br>**Not Important and Not Urgent**<br>**Eliminate**<br>A waste of time and life |

**Figure 6**

The priority matrix was popularized by Stephen Covey some years ago, but the oldest reference I have found dates to World War II, giving credit to then General Eisenhower for originally developing the idea. The matrix is a powerful way to take a quick look at what will truly make a difference in your life and in your thought patterns.

A priority matrix can provide a snapshot of your life, making visible what's on your plate, so to speak. It will bring to light the things and activities consuming your time—because where your time goes, so goes your life. Or put another way, what consumes your time consumes your life.

You can do a priority snapshot for a day, a week, a month, a year, and more. As you develop this picture of how your life is being spent, you position yourself to think about life in a new way. As you see and consider, you process the information needed to move forward.

Let's develop the picture and consider what to do next. Using the priority matrix form in **Exercise 5 of Section 3**, identify the things in the last few weeks that have consumed most of your time. As each item comes to mind, determine whether it is important or not, and whether it is urgent or not. Once you make this determination, record your answer in the appropriate quadrant. As a guide, take a look at the examples in the form.

The following is an example of items from one of my old priority matrixes:

**Important** and **Urgent**

- Give all tax filing documents for the year to accountant before the end of the month
- Finish the quarterly draft report for review by next Friday
- Take sick pet to the vet ASAP
- Schedule trip to management meeting by the end of the month
- Call our largest customer about production issues as soon as information is received from plant

**Important** but **Not Urgent**

- Spend time with my wife each morning before going to work
- Running men's group at church
- Monthly budget review with my wife

- Vacation planning for the remainder of the year
- Repair ceiling in my home office caused by a small roof leak
- Keep tabs on work email at least twice a day
- Maintain my five-morning-per-week workout schedule

**Not Important** but **Urgent**

- Some work email
- John's regular requests for help, due to him waiting until the last minute
- Responding to unimportant phone calls at work
- Phone constantly ringing

**Not Important** and **Not Urgent**

- Constantly checking personal email
- Answering every phone call
- Surfing the web for new camera and lens
- Majority of my personal email
- Drop-ins at the office
- Many unproductive phone calls each day

Let's now consider what you have by discussing each quadrant.

## **Important** and **Urgent: IU**

The items you have listed as both important and urgent will certainly require time from you and should be paid great attention. We often respond quickly to items in the IU quadrant. For example, one of the items in my IU quadrant emerged when one of my important clients had a sudden opportunity and needed my services immediately. Because of the situation and the relationship, I rescheduled a number of things so I could help them.

While there are times when unexpected things like this happen, there are other times when something winds up in this column because of inattention. This happened to me recently when I kept putting off dealing with an important item: a vacation trip. Although I'd had months to do this, I waited too long to buy the airline tickets. Suddenly, I was faced with a looming deadline, fully realizing the airfare would cost more because I had kept putting it off. Unfortunately, I not only paid more for the flights, but I was no longer able to get my seating preferences—all because I procrastinated.

## **Important** but **Not Urgent: INU**

The important but not urgent quadrant contains mostly items that help us create more value in our lives. Because of this, I often refer to this as the *creating quadrant*.

One of the big items in many baby boomers' INU quadrants is that of retirement and other such planning—things like continued education, exercising to maintain or improve health, making marriage a priority, and spending time with kids and others we care about. Pay particular attention to the things in this quadrant, as they are often important to our health and well-being, as well as long-term satisfaction in life. They might not be urgent, but they cannot and should not be postponed indefinitely.

## **Not Important** but **Urgent : NIU**

The not important yet urgent quadrant is one of *opportunity*. By recognizing what is in this quadrant—and then making decisions to either delegate, say no, or otherwise dispose of them—you can add time and reduce stress in your life.

Many times, the things in this quadrant are being imposed on you because of someone else's lack of planning. For example,

I once had a co-worker who would come to me several times a year at the eleventh hour asking for help on something he had procrastinated on. After helping him a few times, and dealing with the stress it created, it dawned on me that it was *his* problem and not *mine*.

Up to this point he knew he could count on me to bail him out. By doing so, I was literally enabling his bad habit. The relationship eventually became strained because of my inability to say no, and because I could not let him be fully responsible for the consequences of his own actions (or in this case, inactions).

Other things that wind up in the NIU quadrant are meetings we have no business attending; allowing constant interruptions from the telephone; and the inability to just say no to certain requests.

If there is an area of your life where you could put procrastination to good use, benefitting you in the long run, it is in this and the next quadrant.

## **Not Important** and **Not Urgent: NINU**

The not important and not urgent quadrant consists of *true* time-wasters. When I have things in this quadrant to work on—which I always do—the effort I waste here would be put to good use if I just shifted it to better things.

Eliminate everything you can in this quadrant. While downtime might seem to go naturally in the NINU, we all *need* some downtime. In fact, it can be helpful to add some downtime into our not urgent but important quadrant, to allow us to rest and recharge.

To become more conscious and deliberate of the amount of downtime we need can be valuable and allow us to make better use of our time.

Take some time now to do **Exercise 5 of Section 3**, where you will find the full version with an example of the priority matrix.

## Learn to Say No

To gain control of your time, and therefore your life, you must focus on what is important and what can truly make a difference in the larger scheme of things. In fact, as valuable as time is—and considering the time wasted in an average person's life—it is almost incomprehensible that we give time away with so little thought.

Yet that is reality and that is life. We are still human, after all, and what is important to one person may be totally unimportant to another.

I have a simple litmus test for where I spend my life. I regularly ask myself, "Does this activity add to my life experience, or does it add to my relationship(s)?" Of course, the opposite is true, too: "Does it take away from my life or from my relationship(s)?"

One of the most valuable skills you can learn, when coming to the realization of where your time is going, is the ability to say no to things that, even though they temporarily make you feel good, simply waste your time and life.

Saying NO makes more room in your life to say YES to those things that truly add value to your life. Remember, this is *your* life that you are living. You only get one shot at it. How do *you* want to live it?

Do you want to control what you can, or give the control away to others? Do you value your time and therefore your life? Are you making the right decisions by using your time to add to life, or allowing it to be taken away? It's your choice.

An example of this is when you're guilted into committing to something that you're not passionate about doing. Perhaps you're experienced in accounting, and friends ask if you can do their taxes for them.

While you might want to say yes for the sake of your friendship, if taking on this project takes time away from your wife and kids—which has been on your not urgent but important list—it might end up taking away more from your life than adding to it.

Remember, just because someone asks for something doesn't mean you have to say yes. Give each request thoughtful consideration, and then make a decision that most benefits your long-term goals. If nurturing your marriage is most important, that takes precedence. Knowing your real priorities can help you make the best decision for when to say yes or no.

As Peter Drucker once stated so well: "People are effective because they say 'no,' because they say, 'this isn't for me.'" To live the best life possible, learn to say no to the not important and not urgent.

## Expectation Vs. Intention

We've been talking a lot about your goals, your priorities, and your patterns. Now it's time to frame the results you have created so far by talking about expectations.

Let's take something important to most of us: the money we earn. Ask yourself two questions:

- Do I expect an increase in my pay?
- What can I do with the intention to increase my income?

Look at those questions closely. Which one has more power to get you your desired results?

Think about anything else you want to happen. First phrase it as "I expect this." Now reword that same comment: "I intend to do such and such to make certain I get this." Again, which has more power—the expectation or the intention?

You'll notice a significant difference between expectations and intentions. An *expectation* is anticipating something to happen, whereas *intention* is a determination to act to *make it happen.*

Now, there's also a difference between realistic versus unrealistic expectations—but either way, an expectation is passive, not something you act on and do.

You must be active to deliberately create what you want.

When you take a realistic expectation and develop it into an intention, you put legs on it. Your intention is something that will be done. You'll work on it and take action on it as you move toward achieving it.

Another way to look at expectation versus intention is:

**Expectation** – Something that is coming to us. We are waiting for it.

**Intention** – Something we are going toward. We are accomplishing it.

An expectation is simply an assumption; to expect is to *assume* something will happen. It's a *passive* state of mind. And you know what they say about assuming...

An intention drives action, making it happen. It's an *active* state of mind.

Does this make sense? If not, reread it again and again until it does. In the simple difference between expectation and intention lies the secret to achievement. Intention involves maturity and the acceptance of responsibility. It's not just about what happens to you; it's about what you *do,* not what someone else does.

Here are a few quick examples to help illustrate the difference:

- I *expect* my wife to love me. I *intend* to love my wife.
- I *expect* the promotion to happen. I *intend* to work for the promotion.
- I *expect* them to treat me with respect. I *intend* to act respectfully to earn their respect.
- I *expect* to win the lottery, so I won't have to worry about retirement. I *intend* to work and save so I have enough to retire when I am older.
- I *expect* Social Security to be there when I retire. I *intend* to save enough money to retire without government assistance.
- I *expect* I'll be able to provide for my family. I *intend* to provide for my family.

## The One Thing?

So why go through all of this effort? Want to know the secret of the most successful and significant people that have ever lived? It's this: They know how to focus on one thing and use it as the lens through which they do everything they do.

Think about it. You can do one thing very well if you put all your effort into it. And as we mentioned before about multi-tasking, if you attempt to spread your effort between two things, you might come up short with one or both. When you distribute that same time and effort between three or more goals—well, you get the picture.

Going after the *one thing* you really want can be a difficult choice, yet your results from focusing on one thing can produce a great return. Dividing your attention between two things equally does not necessarily result in double the return; if anything, you will likely find you will reap *less* from each. And with three or more demands, results diminish even further.

When you are working on one thing, you will usually do it well. But life doesn't always cooperate when we're trying to focus. We suddenly have more than one urgent task, plus email to attend to, plus drop-ins, office chat, meetings, and on and on.

Have you ever gotten to the end of a day and wondered what happened to it, and feel you accomplished nothing? This seems to be the new normal for too many of us. I used to come into the office on Saturdays because, when no one else was there, I could get so much more work done. Yet I did this at the expense of spending time with my family. That was not a good trade at all.

We're doing this review on multi-tasking and focus for a bigger reason this time. Think of what you could accomplish if you could just focus on one thing, even for a short, concentrated time, with absolutely zero distractions or other obligations.

You don't learn to play an instrument very well if you don't focus on it. If it's true that to become an expert on something you must spend 10,000 hours doing or studying it—well, that's a lot of effort in one direction, to say the least.

During a typical year, you spend about 2,000 hours at work if you work forty hours a week, fifty weeks a year. In exchange for that huge outlay of time, what are you becoming an expert at? I'll let you think on that one for a bit.

Look back at your answers in Chapter 5 and ask again, "What do I really want in life?" Considering the mortality rate on earth continues to stand at 100 percent—meaning we all eventually die—what is it that will make you thankful for how you lived your life?

This is a serious personal question, of course. But what if you could discover that one thing that matters most to you? You could begin your journey in that direction, rather than wandering aimlessly, chasing whatever, hoping for the best. What could you achieve?

Wandering in the wrong direction takes up your most precious resource—time. To move forward intentionally, purposefully, toward what will enrich your life, you must *deliberately* make the best use of this precious resource of time. Isn't that what you want?

I'll give you another secret to moving forward and creating more significance in life. Most people are looking for someone they can get behind. If you have a strong enough purpose, and you focus on the one thing you have discovered that makes life truly meaningful for you, others will want to help you. They will get behind you and follow you, and the impact you make while on this earth both now and after you leave will be far greater.

After all, who follows someone who has no clear direction and purpose in life? Who follows someone who wanders around aimlessly from day to day? Sure, some may. But do you want to be responsible for that?

What about those who see you and your life and want to follow your example? Wow. This is heavy stuff, isn't it? And it is reality.

All of us—especially those of us in leadership—have a serious responsibility to others. How we live our lives, who we are, and who we are becoming has an effect on others—whether we want it to or not.

What we do and don't do, the direction we travel, the words we write and say—all of these things impact others. We have a responsibility to be purposeful about these things. distractions from what is really important reduces your purpose and meaning, and the hard truth of it is that it's irresponsible.

So, what is the one thing you can focus your life on that will make the biggest difference in what you do, in who you are, and in who you're becoming? Be real when you ask yourself this. See reality. As master creator Robert Fritz once said: "Reality is an acquired taste." To not see reality is to either remain ignorant or to lie to yourself. Which is better to do?

> *"Do not many of us who fail to achieve big things ... fail because we lack concentration—the art of concentrating the mind on the thing to be done at the proper time and to the exclusion of everything else?"*
>
> — John D. Rockefeller

Let's look at a few examples of people who clearly knew their one thing, in their own words.

**Thomas Edison**, the prolific inventor, one stated: "My desire is to do everything within my power to further free the people from drudgery and create the largest possible measures of happiness and prosperity."

**Mother Teresa**, who touched not just the lives of the people of Calcutta, India, but people all around the globe, said, "Spread love everywhere you go. Let no one ever come to you without leaving happier."

**Steve Jobs**, world-class entrepreneur, famously said, "Apple is about people who think 'outside the box,' people who want to use computers to help them change the world, to help them create things that make a difference, and not just to get a job done."

**Billy Graham**, preached to live audiences of more than 210 million people in 185 countries, with an estimated lifetime audience, including radio and television broadcasts, topping 2.2 billion people. Billy was a friend to many famous celebrities and presidents—and was chosen as one of the ten most-admired men in the world a record-breaking fifty-nine times in the Gallup poll. Billy once said of his ministry: "My calling is to preach the love of God and the forgiveness of God and the fact that He does forgive us. That's what the cross is all about, what the resurrection is all about, that's the gospel."

**Abraham Lincoln**, our country's sixteenth President, said about his very successful life: "I am not bound to win, but I am bound to be true. I am not bound to succeed, but I am bound to live up to what light I have. I must stand with anybody that stands right, and stand with him while he is right, and part with him when he goes wrong."

From these quotes, you can see that these famous people chose underlying principles for their lives, rather than material goals. Once you find your one thing, align everything you do to it. Use the one thing as your aiming point. Whatever you do, do it in order to move toward this underlying principle.

Carefully consider those things that move you away from your goal or throw off your trajectory, and don't act on these things. In some cases, you might need to stop the distractions that pull you off course.

Your journey will be one step at a time, but you must try to take each step in the right direction. To take one step left, or right, or backwards increases the amount of time it will cost you to get to your goal. Missteps use up that most precious and valuable resource: your time.

Now this may sound contradictory, but guess what? Your *one thing* might be refined over time. It might even change! Then again, it might not. But be open to the idea that what you find as your one thing today might evolve into something else over time.

The key here is that simply finding your one thing now will define your path. You might find that it puts you on a very different path than you were on before.

Knowing what truly matters to you will shape how you see things, allowing you to have a clearer vision. It will provide direction for your questions, thoughts, and actions.

When you focus more intensely on what really matters, your results will be proportionate. Life will have more purpose and become more meaningful. Without the one thing in your vision and in your heart, at least some of your time will certainly be wasted.

Don't let your passion or time slip through your fingers. Keep searching for your one thing until you are sure you know what it is.

## CHAPTER SUMMARY

- The priority matrix can be used for making sense of what to do with your time.
- Say no to the unimportant.
- Expectation is passive, intention is active.
- Focusing on the one thing that matters most to you will help guide you where you need to be.

**Questions and activities to deepen my learning from this chapter:**

- What can I work on that is in my INU quadrant today?
- I will practice saying no to requests that do not align with my desired outcomes.
- What expectations should I change to intentions?
- What is my one thing?
- I will complete **Exercise 5 - Prioritizing in Section 3**.

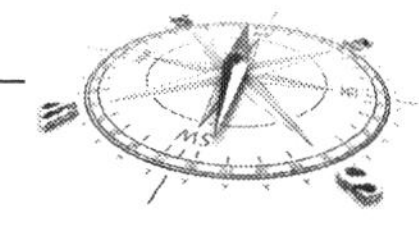

CHAPTER 7

# Acting in New Ways

Are you leading your life or letting life just happen to you?

You are always following someone, whether it is yourself or someone else. So who is leading your life?

You make all of the decisions in your life, good, bad, and indifferent. But it isn't always clear who or what you are following, is it? Are your many choices each day made deliberately, haphazardly, or with serious thought? Perhaps a bit of each?

Ultimately, you bear the responsibility for your own life; you create the result of the life you live, by the decisions you make. Whether you try your hardest or give up immediately, it's your life and your choice of how you lead it. Even following others is a leadership choice!

The bottom line is: To make good decisions in your life, you must accept responsibility for yourself. You must take the lead.

If you accept full and complete responsibility for yourself, and for all of your decisions, you become the leader in your own life. That's one definition of true maturity.

If you do not accept responsibility for yourself, well … who are you? Are you just a victim of circumstances?

It's true that terrible things can happen to us. We can be a victim of a crime or a tragedy. In those cases, it's reasonable to say we have been *victimized*. However, it's important not to make that experience part of your identity which keeps you in a mindset of weakness and helplessness. Instead, choose to take charge of your life and move toward what you need and want. To be a victim is to be controlled by outside forces. Instead of being a victim, become a victor and create your future.

## To Not Choose IS a Choice

It's true—not making a choice *is* a choice. It is a choice to not choose.

Every time we learn something new, we have a decision to make, and we can make it consciously or unconsciously. This is especially true when we learn something helpful.

We can decide to act on new information or decide to just let it be. Letting it be is a choice to not act. As philosopher William James put it: "When you have to make a choice and don't make it, that in itself is a choice."

Another thing to recognize about decisions and choices is that they take us toward or away from something. To learn some useful information and choose to act on it takes us *toward* a new result. To let it be is to move away from what we have learned, or to remain where we are.

If all of life is moving forward, into the future, how do we reconcile forward movement with indecisive stagnation? The answer is to not accept moving backwards or the status quo, and then to determine what you can do and *act* on it.

The priority matrix introduced in the last chapter allows you to consider whether something is worth doing. If a task lands in the top half of the matrix, it *is* worth considering.

Of course, your time-management decisions are subjective, but that subjectivity is necessary. After all, each life and each person's goals are unique. The decision you make should be truly yours and not come from the pressure of someone else's influence or control.

Let's take another look at an example we discussed earlier: interruptions.

Controlling interruptions leads to producing better work and enhancing productivity while diminishing stress. To act on the decision to control interruptions, you first must see it and the opportunity that exists, deliberate on it, and then make the choice to begin taking actions that lead to reaping greater fulfillment.

Remember Seneca's comment back in Chapter 2? "Luck is what happens when preparation meets opportunity." In other words, the more we prepare ourselves, the more opportunities we see. Many times, the only reason we see an opportunity is because we have done the preparation needed. Unless you are actively studying and learning, you might not even see or understand that an opportunity exists.

Changing business trends can represent an opportunity, but only if vendors notice and are prepared to respond. An example of this is the changing economic climate of online shopping.

When retailers bury their heads in the sand, ignoring shopping trends, they're unaware of growing opportunities to adjust their business practices to compete in the new market.

But when they see and think about the changing trends, they can act to adjust their business in order to take advantage of new market opportunities.

We can see examples of businesses that took each of these approaches in the past several years, and see where it got them. Businesses that incorporated online shopping are thriving. Those that didn't see it coming, or didn't respond in time, are now filing for bankruptcy.

There are always new ways to grow, but you have to look for them!

When you make a choice to act on something you've learned about, you move toward better preparing yourself to see *even greater* opportunity.

The principle of preparation applies to every area of life. Imagine if a person has done the preparation necessary to become a doctor. Because of their preparation and understanding of anatomy, they see things a normal person cannot. That's how they can diagnose and treat an illness.

If a lawyer doesn't know the ins and outs of the law, how could he represent you in court? If an accountant or engineer does not have understanding beyond basic math, what good would they be at their jobs?

The same is true even for parenting. Unless you spend time studying the subject, or at least talking to people with more experience than you have, how can you see the opportunities to become a better parent?

What if we see or learn of an opportunity, but can't decide if it's worth pursuing? Perhaps it's a good choice for some people—but you are you, and I am me. We must always give ourselves permission to do what is in line with our values, our dreams and hopes, our desires, and to our concept of fulfillment. Not every opportunity will fit the bill.

Finally, there can be instances in which making a good choice moves us away from something. Sometimes, we find ourselves in negative circumstances. We can make a choice to move away from toxic people, to not read or watch things that are inappropriate, or to not overdo something that might end up hurting us. The purpose of this book is not to explore these circumstances; however, we cannot neglect their reality in life.

You always make a choice, whether you act or not, and the choice is always yours. As Aristotle said: "For what is the best choice, for each individual is the highest it is possible for him to achieve."

## Maturity is Responsibility

Self-leadership can transform your ability to act on what you want in life because it's founded in *responsibility*.

Who is responsible for your life? If you're a free person living in a free country, take a look in the mirror.

Albert Schweitzer once said that "man must cease attributing his problems to his environment, and learn again to exercise his will, his personal responsibility." In other words, don't blame your circumstances; take responsibility for *yourself*.

Have you ever stopped to consider what personal responsibility is? Many years back, in Edwin Cole's *Maximized Manhood* book, I read: "Maturity doesn't come with age but begins with the acceptance of responsibility." I deeply considered this statement, and it continues to ring true to me today. My level of maturity is directly related to my acceptance of responsibility.

This means my growth as a human being is my responsibility, and isn't dependent on circumstances or people or whatever else there may be. The more I become responsible, the more I mature.

What are some ways in which we can grow? Let's apply the S.T.A.R. Approach to it and find out.

First, I must See that there is a direct link between my ability to accept responsibility and my growth as a person. If I don't take responsibility for it, who will?

Perhaps when I was a child, my parents had some say—but I am an adult now. Why would I want to become a child again and allow someone else to force something on me, essentially taking away my ability to grow?

Once I see the link between maturity and responsibility, I can engage in Thinking and studying what is important to me. As my thinking expands, so does my ability to understand what Actions I can take. Here I can choose those actions that are best suited to who I am. As I act in these new ways, I will Reap new results.

Think about this. When you take responsibility for yourself, you put first things first. This might require you to put off some of the things you desire in order to spend that time on something else.

If a young man puts aside personal recreation time so he can spend more time with his wife and children, for example, he is not only becoming more mature, but also he's investing in the most important thing in his life: his closest relationships.

At the end of your life, the reward you reap will be great, because you **saw** what was important, considered (**thought** about) what was best, **acted** responsibly by doing what you knew was right, then **reaped** an outcome different than most.

When a young woman **understands** (sees) that if she **studies** (thinks) hard, **goes** to college (acts on it), and **lands** a promising job (reaps), it started when she took the responsibility to apply herself and to do the work required to learn. She made the right choices, resulting in a great job with a promising career.

It might not be that the two people I just wrote about are necessarily smarter than everyone else. It is that they accepted responsibility, saw what was important, and applied themselves to do the right thing. They were diligent in their efforts, realizing results that matter on which they can continue to build.

Sometimes, taking responsibility can be a joint effort. When a husband and wife notice (see) the value of what they do *not* spend, requiring them to be thoughtful (think), and realize it's what they *save* that makes the difference; and they become diligent (act) with their finances throughout their lives, being responsible with each dollar, the results (reap) can be significant.

As a result of their collaboration, they can end up retiring when they want, comfortably, rather than joining the majority who will struggle or barely get by. This husband and wife saw what was important to them, considered it thoroughly, made the necessary plans and budgets, and reaped the results they desired. It could only have happened because they took responsibility.

## React, Respond, Create?

Perhaps you're familiar with the saying that it is better to respond than to react. True. To *react* is essentially to do something without thought.

One reason people react is that they do not see or understand what is driving them beneath the surface. The cause is often biological.

It's well established in neuroscience that our emotions and many of our reactions originate in the limbic portion of the brain, while our rational thinking is tied to the cerebral cortex of the brain.

The limbic system operates hundreds of times more quickly than the cerebral cortex. This speedy reaction is important in life-threatening situations, when you have no time to think and must react quickly.

However, when it comes to ordinary tasks, it is best to allow the rational, thinking portion of the brain to have time to process the feelings and emotions of the limbic system so you can choose your response more deliberately.

Think about a time when you became angry, such as when someone cut you off in traffic, nearly causing an accident. If you're like many of us, you probably reacted quickly with an outburst of anger, which might have included a few choice words. That was a reaction!

The same thing can happen when someone says something that triggers you. Your limbic system goes into its fight-flight-freeze mode and you may hastily react, perhaps speaking sharply or yelling at them. Alternatively, you might want to run or shut down.

Many people go through life in a reactive mode much of the time, reacting to things without thinking. What quality of results do you think they reap?

How can you move to a more thoughtful manner of responding rather than reacting? First, you must recognize that the limbic or emotional center of your brain can be hijacked. This will cause you to quickly react, even when it would be better not to.

In high-stress situations, such as in an accident or when you're under extreme pressure, you can expect to react quickly and not necessarily appropriately.

But not *everything* is an emergency—is it? What about other areas of your life, such as what you do with your time? Are you allowing circumstances or the environment around you to dictate what you do—or do you pause, look at the situation, and make a thoughtful decision?

Responding requires that you think and make a better decision than you would normally make in a purely reactive mode. If you give yourself time to think before you react, you will most likely get a better result.

Responding in a thoughtful way, rather than reacting, is part of being more responsible. Responding means you took the time to consider and weigh the options and then chose the best one.

To become the leader in your life, you must at least reach the level of being able to respond. Reacting is allowing someone or something else—outside circumstances—to control you and your destiny.

To respond means you take the leadership reins and become responsible to yourself and your principles. To respond is to take the time needed to allow the rational part of your brain to catch up with the limbic system, so you can make a decision that will serve your higher desires.

The better the quality of the questions you ask yourself, the better your response will be, and the better the outcome. Again, you must see what is happening, think about it, and then act in a way that will deliver a better result.

While responding is better than reacting, there is an even higher level of self-leadership: that of creating. As with responding, you give thought to the best options you see in a situation. But in creating, you take it to a deeper level, delving into what you really want.

Simply responding is not going to provide you with what you may need at the deepest level. Responses, even highly mature ones, can be rooted in many things and can sometimes stifle your ability to create.

If you simply respond based on what you already know, or based on how life and people have conditioned your thinking, it can be hard to be creative.

Rather than saying, "I want to begin saving money for retirement, so I'm going to invest heavily in my retirement plan," ask yourself better questions. Is my retirement plan the best possible way to increase my long-term savings? If you apply your creativity to a situation, you might come up with something entirely different, something beyond the obvious.

Take this book, for example. This book is a way for me to share a part of myself, impart wisdom on others, and create a lasting legacy for what has helped me succeed in life. In a way, creating this book is part of my retirement plan—not just monetarily, but to leave a mark on the world. But it took self-leadership to write these words!

This higher level of leadership, personal or otherwise, is about vision and direction. First, you must see what you want to create as clearly as possible. Then you must take action and keep making course corrections to stay on the right path, going in the right direction.

In fact, leadership is always about *direction*. What you do determines the direction you go and where you wind up.

Allowing yourself to be primarily in a reactive mode will take you in one direction and give you one set of results. To be more thoughtful and responsive will take you in another direction.

To create something new will bring entirely new results, in an entirely different direction.

The choice is yours. React and be led or lead by being more deliberate in creating what you want.

Here are some examples of reacting, responding, and creating:

Someone cuts you off in traffic. Rather than allow it to trigger you, you pause, take control of your breathing, calm yourself, and become thankful that there was no accident. This is a more effective response to the situation.

What can you create in a situation like this? If you use the near-accident to strengthen your ability to pause and not be triggered, to become thankful instead of resentful, and to reframe the situation (maybe the other driver is having a really bad day and didn't see you), you begin to create something totally new.

If a near-accident makes you more determined to stay alert in traffic and pay closer attention on the road, you're going in an even better direction.

When you pause and think of a careful response, those adrenaline-spiked reactions dissipate completely. Each time something triggers you, you use it as an opportunity to improve your ability to create a new way to act and bring less stress and more joy into your life.

Or, let's say you are feeling pressured because you are getting older and haven't saved enough for retirement. Instead of just reacting with worry—which has known ill effects on your health—you decide to notice the trigger, slow down, and give some thought as to what to do.

Your thoughtful response is to try to save as much as you can and keep on working. To take this to the next level of creating what you want, perhaps you can enlist the help of others—a financial planner, for example—and take up learning more about the subject of growing the investments you have.

A truly creative approach to retirement might include learning more about what it will take to live the lifestyle you really want to live, evaluating cost-effective locations to live in once you do retire, or thinking about retirement-friendly part-time jobs.

If you're a business professional, maybe you'll branch out and start consulting, using your expertise. This creativity might give you more scheduling flexibility to accommodate your retired life.

The options are endless, but you'll need the skill of thoughtful self-leadership in order to envision opportunities and thus see the entire situation in a different light to create something else entirely.

Any form of creativity is bound to give you a better result than simply reacting by worrying.

To move from reacting to responding to creating, you simply need to pause, think, and develop a vision of what you really want—and then begin the work of moving in that direction.

You can create what you want if you are willing to become responsible and lead yourself in a way beyond where reacting or responding will take you.

## Who Are You and What Are You Becoming?

Before moving on, let's look at one more thing about taking charge as the leader in your life. That thing is nothing less than *who you are*.

Personal leadership comes from who you are and who you are becoming. To lead is to create. To create more value for yourself and others, you must continue to grow and change.

To lead requires clarity about what you wish to create that you can articulate, that can be seen (your vision). The more clearly you *see* what you want to create, the more *intentional* you become and the more decisive your actions are. You then move toward creating something different, something new. Sounds simple? Yet it's not easy.

The best advice I have to improving your ability to lead is this: Become *more than you are*. Make a conscious decision to take charge of creating your own future.

Work on yourself, expand and deepen your thinking, gain clarity, and then do it. Leading is not just about a position, such as becoming president of a company. You can lead in every area of life. You can lead your family, your peers, your bosses, the people that work for you, your board, in your church, literally anywhere and everywhere.

The responsibility is yours to become more than you are today, to grow and not allow atrophy to set in.

## CHAPTER SUMMARY

- You are the leader in your life, if you choose to be.
- To *not choose* is still a choice.
- The more responsibility you take, the more mature you are.
- You can choose to react, respond, or create.

**Questions and activities to deepen my learning from this chapter:**

- Who is the leader in my life? Asked another way, who am I following?
- Am I making conscious choices to create what I want, or simply reacting or responding to circumstances?
- How would I rate my maturity on a scale of 1 to 10, with 10 being the most mature?
- Who and what am I becoming?

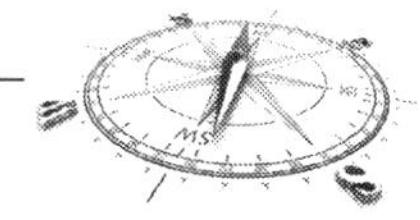

CHAPTER 8

# Reaping New Results

Here comes the Reaper! No, I'm not talking about the Grim Reaper. I'm talking about you—the one who has the most to gain, the one who can reap the most by taking action.

The more you apply the S.T.A.R. Approach, the more you'll envision a brighter future unfolding before you. And it's easy to get caught up in the future. But once in a while, we have to hit the pause button.

The most important thing to do when you act and create something new is to stop and appreciate what has been accomplished. As we have said, what you appreciate, *appreciates*—(and conversely, what you don't appreciate, *depreciates*).

When you have a win or success, it is important to take some time and be thankful for what you have accomplished. This will make success more a part of who you are and who you are becoming.

Don't allow your victories to slip by! Why do we dwell on our failures and ignore our successes? It's human nature, but you can learn a better way.

Let's discuss some things that can help you appreciate—or get in the way of appreciating—what you reap.

## What Do You Say When You Talk to Yourself?

Who do you suppose is your worst enemy? He's been with you as long as you can remember. As cartoonist Walt Kelly's character Pogo once said, "We have met the enemy and he is us."

Yes, there is part of each of us that keeps us from becoming more of who we are capable of becoming. It's our own self-imposed limitations. Where does this part of us come from? Let's try to make sense of it all.

Think about what goes on in your thoughts that no one else can see—the doubts, the fears, the cares and concerns, the good, the bad, and the ugly. Each is a part of who you are. Each expands or restricts the life you live.

I've come to see these parts of myself in new ways as I age. For much of my life, I was unaware of them, thus unable to see or stop them. I did not realize they even existed until I learned of them from someone else.

Once I began developing the ability to see these parts of myself, and to think about and reflect on them, I started to take steps to change them. This has allowed me to develop control over these thoughts, rather than being controlled by them.

A few years back, a shift happened in my thoughts about these different parts of me. While I originally viewed some parts of myself as "the enemy," I've now come to see them for what they are. Most have been with me since I was a child. They're just parts that have not matured well.

There is a part of me that fears public speaking, and a part that tells me I'm not good enough. They are like a small child crying "Wolf!" when there is no wolf.

These parts of me have not grown up, but they continue to voice their concerns. I understand now that they will hinder my progress if I allow them. But why? Why do these parts of me do what they do?

Let's extend this concept further. These parts of me actually have their own voice. Have you ever had a thought come to you inside your mind that seemed to *speak* to you?

There is much research on this that indicates each of us have these "voices" inside us. In fact, there are whole systems of therapy based on them. Check out the latest research by simply doing an internet search on internal voices and neuroscience. You'll be amazed at the work that exists in this area.

These voices will say things like, "You can't do that," or "You're not qualified to accomplish anything like that," or "If you do that, you will make a fool of yourself." Your inner voice can be highly critical: "You don't have the education that so-and-so does, so what makes you think you can do something like that?" And on and on they go.

For the most part, I have found that many of my parts, or voices, trace back to a younger Bill Abbate, often from my childhood or young adult years. At first, I despised these voices. I was angry that I would tell myself such things. But now I've come to understand them differently.

Rather than think of my critical inner voices as destructive and condescending, I now see how they came from a part of me that served me in some way at one time. I outgrew them, and they no longer serve me, but they still exist.

As I examined each of these voices, I realized many came from fear. I discovered these younger, undeveloped or underdeveloped parts of me had been trying to protect me in their own way. They want to keep me from experiencing hurt, failure, embarrassment, and so forth. In their own way, they try to serve me.

Before I could see these parts of myself, I regularly fell prey to their input. When they warned or criticized, I *listened,* and I sometimes allowed them to control my thoughts and emotions.

What's a person to do when part of his own brain seems intent on sabotaging his future? First, recognize that these parts or voices exist; come to **see** each of them.

Instead of being subject to your inner voices, make them subject to you. Put another way, see each of them as part of your divided self and as an object that you can examine by thinking and reflecting. Hold it up and look at it from different angles or perspectives. We'll talk more about Subject-Object Theory in Chapter 9.

By doing this, I recognized early on that these parts of me imposed limitations on what I was able to do *only* so long as I allowed them to have influence on me. Until I could see them clearly, they influenced me greatly. But I was always stronger than they were.

The limitations I imposed on myself, which I now refer to as *self-limiting beliefs,* are real. I have yet to meet a person that doesn't have some. I have, however, met many people who, like me, did not realize that they had self-imposed limitations.

What are the sources of these self-defeating thoughts? Do the following sentence-completion exercise to unearth as many as you can. Try to remember what people in your life, especially your early life, have said to you. If you don't have a clear memory of their words, try to imagine what they *would* say, to represent their attitude toward you.

- Parents
  - Why do you have to be so ________________?
  - Why can't you be good like ___________?
  - You'll never be as smart as _______________.
  - If you don't get your grades up, you'll never ______.
  - You embarrass me when you ______.
  - Quit being so __________.
  - You'll never amount to _________________.
- Our siblings
  - You're _______________.
  - I hate when you ______________.
  - Because of you, I have to ___________.
- Teachers
  - You're not good enough at ______________________.
  - People like you grow up to be ___________.
  - You'll never be able to ________.
- Fellow students
  - Hey (offensive name) ___________.
  - You're not _________________.
  - I don't want you on my ___________.
  - You're so ____________.
- Spouse
  - A good husband/wife would _______________.
  - You're a lousy _______________.
  - You'll never be successful at _______________.
  - You don't care about _______________.

- Society in general
    - You're too __________.
    - You'll never be successful if you aren't __________.
    - Only _________ people are healthy.
    - Something's wrong if you aren't married by _______.
    - You have to go to _________________ be successful.
    - You have to get/become ___________________.
    - If you don't have a/this ____________, you haven't made it.
    - You must have a career in ______________ to be successful.
    - You must obey all ___________________.
    - You have to own ____________________ to be happy.
    - You must _________________________ to be happy.
- Yourself
    - I'll never be ______________.
    - I always wind up __________________.
    - I can't do it because __________________.
    - I'm just not ___________________.
    - I'm much too ___________________.
    - I don't have enough ___________________.
    - I don't know enough about ______________________ to be successful.
    - I'm not ____________ enough.
    - I'm only _________________.

The above are only a few examples of where your critical inner thoughts come from. Do you hear any echoes in what was said to you, way back then? Are you still saying those things to yourself?

I want you to notice these inner voices, which can originate from sources external and internal, depending on the way we've been conditioned. I'm sure you can come up with others on your own.

Whenever you tell yourself you can't or shouldn't do something, examine your thinking and ask where it is coming from. Which voice is speaking to you, and where does it come from?

When you have any negative thoughts, ask the same thing: What voice is speaking and where does it come from? Then challenge what it says, and don't stop until you have an answer.

This also applies to any fear or doubt you have. Don't give up. Inquire within yourself and ask, "What CAN I do?"

Why is it important to recognize these sources? There is power in seeing, understanding, and recognizing where a voice originates because then you can decide if its message is still valid for you.

If you allow these voices to go unchecked, there is little you can do about them. They can control your thoughts and affect your emotions. They can be the source of much frustration.

Yet when you can identify where a critical inner voice is coming from, you can make your own choice as to whether to believe it. You can move from letting it control you to you controlling it. You can make a deliberate choice about what to do with the information you are given. Should you accept or reject it?

You can choose to become mindful of what is happening, or mindlessly allow other things—including the voices in your own head—to control you. You can be mindful of, or be mindless in, your daily thoughts. Which do you prefer?

When your eyes are opened to your self-imposed limitations, you can begin to thoughtfully examine them. You can *take responsibility* for them, which helps you grow in maturity.

Since these limitations are in our minds, and there are potentially many, what can you do to see them more clearly? To answer this question and make them visible, I suggest you pause now and work through **Exercises 6 and 7 in Section 3**. These exercises will help you draw a contrast between self-empowering beliefs and self-limiting beliefs.

Why is all this self-examination part of our study of reaping? Think about it this way. If you fail to recognize the rewards you have earned, why would you continue to see, think, and act in new ways? Why would you continue to move forward and win in life if you don't take time to enjoy it?

The better you know yourself, the more you can appreciate your accomplishments. Only by questioning and ultimately silencing your critical inner voice can you let your accomplishments lead to more and even better accomplishments.

If you desire, you can change self-limiting beliefs into real opportunities. First, you need to **see** the self-limiting belief. Then you must give it some real **thought**, examining as many perspectives as you can, even enlisting others in the process of developing more perspectives. Once you have done this, you can **act** on the decisions and choices that will support what you really want. This will literally change the outcome you **reap**/receive.

Remember that these self-limiting beliefs come from somewhere inside, likely a part of yourself that is fearful and trying to protect you in some way. For me, the fear of public speaking began when I was just a child.

I well remember when I was in the second grade, how I tripped and almost fell onstage during a school play. It was bad enough that I was already uncomfortable, just being in front of so many people.

As I recalled the incident, I remembered how embarrassed I was. I remember the feelings of how all those people in the audience, including my own family, must have thought I was a clumsy loser.

Could a voice from when I was seven still influence me into my twenties like that? You bet. Yet that voice was just trying to keep me from further embarrassment. It was using fear to protect me from ever being in that situation again.

As I advanced in my career, I was put on the spot more and more often to speak. Eventually, I attended a Dale Carnegie course on public speaking and started to read more about the subject to help me overcome my fear. Then I was able to quiet this voice in my head.

Is it gone? Nope. It's still there. Yet I see it so differently now.

Whenever I get nervous, as I prepare to speak to an audience, that seven-year-old part of me still wants to protect me from looking like a fool, from failing. But I now have another part of me that tells me I *can* do it. I *have done* it and have been successful at it many times, as long as I'm prepared.

This more mature part of myself tells me I'm going to do a great job, and I believe it. And it happens.

Even if things don't go perfectly, I have another voice inside that tells me it is okay. I am allowed to make some mistakes. I believe others want me to be successful and not to fail. I am encouraged no matter what happens, and I can even laugh at myself.

Another real-life incident happened when I was around thirty years old and had taken a job that unfortunately conflicted with several of my personal values and beliefs. The job paid well, but the stress I was under felt unbearable.

The conflict between what I wanted and what I needed was just too great. After a year and a half, out of desperation, I resigned.

There I was with my small family, jobless, a thousand miles from my home state. I started looking for more work, but nothing appeared.

My self-imposed limitation—worrying about the uncertainty of being able to find another job—came from my fear of not being able to take care of my family. I was a responsible person, after all. At least, that is what part of me believed at that time.

Yet I hadn't been noticing what my reactions to the pressures were doing to my relationship with my wife. I also missed the fact that she was fully in favor of me leaving the position. She had more faith than I did that we would be okay.

Fear is a harsh taskmaster.

I had failed to realize I did a great job for the company, and that I was very capable. I forgot that there really were other opportunities out there. I was so paralyzed with concern and fear, I could not see myself or my situation clearly.

After a short time of unemployment, a different part of me woke up. I realized that I had risen through the ranks because others thought I had strong skills and capabilities. I started to believe I could do what I set my mind to. I had already proven that in my life.

In no time, I had a job that not only improved my future opportunities, but also paid better, and presented me with greater opportunities for growth!

## Cultivating Your Beliefs and Voices

Let's look a little more deeply at what lies beneath our self-empowering and self-limiting beliefs.

Self-empowering beliefs often come from confidence, while self-limiting beliefs usually come from doubt. When you lack confidence, you often feel fear. It is well known in the field of neuroscience that fear causes the mind to narrow its focus and can severely limit your ability to think rationally.

We are complex creatures with complex minds. Thinking can be experienced as an internal dialogue, although you can think and see different perspectives inside your mind without putting those thoughts into words.

The question is, do you recognize this? Are you awake to it? Do you realize your mind has different parts that often manifest themselves in this internal chatter?

For the sake of simplicity, let's assume you notice that you have these different internal voices and you observe how they relate to what you consciously and unconsciously believe.

Self-empowering beliefs and self-limiting beliefs can each have several voices that want to be recognized and heard. To control them, first you must identify them.

A few internal voices I can easily distinguish are the parts of me that think or speak as the father, the husband, the brother, the friend, the older man, and so on. Depending on what is happening, one or more of these voices will influence my thoughts and what I say, or don't say, both internally and out loud. They each, in part, help define my beliefs.

For example, in some business meetings my "executive voice" may come into play, influencing my thoughts and words and actions. At other times, negative voices will vie for my attention, saying things like, "What gives you the right?" or "How in the world do you think you can do that?"

I have named this fearful part of me my "critical voice." Sometimes it pops up and says, "Don't make a fool of yourself!"

I also have positive voices inside, and I am constantly at work cultivating them to become a larger part of me. When I go out for a run as part of my exercise routine, I say, "This is good for me." When I enter a race, I've developed a part of me that says, "I can do this."

There are times when I get ready to speak in front of a group and I hear myself saying, "You're going to be great." Of course, good preparation helps, so I know my subject well. But I welcome what I call my "voice of confidence."

Now, my "voice of confidence" did not come naturally. I developed it over time. As mentioned earlier, there was a time when I would get in front of a group and be so nervous that if I did not have a lectern to lean on, I felt too weak to stand. How well I remember those times!

What dominated my thoughts back then was pure fear—the thought that I was going to fail and look foolish. I'll admit, it was pretty horrifying to me. Public speaking can be the stuff nightmares are made of.

Eventually, however, with practice and a shift in my mindset, the lack of confidence shrank and I gained the voice of confidence that has so greatly affected my life. Sure, the old negative voices can still linger at times. But now I am able to see them, call them out, and even thank them for trying to protect me. Then I allow them to fade into the background, while I consciously bring forward a part of me that has greater confidence and positivity.

I now understand and accept that these parts of me were parts of my younger self, doing their best in their immature way to serve me by creating doubt and self-limiting beliefs. As I came to see and examine them, and learn from them, their influence and control changed dramatically.

I can now take control away from these self-limiting beliefs and develop another part of me that better serves what I want now.

## Your Worst Enemy is Also Your Best Friend

*"Know that you are your greatest enemy,*
*but also your greatest friend."*
*— Jeremy Taylor*

What makes someone a best friend? For me, it is someone I can trust, who doesn't judge me, who accepts me for who I am, and genuinely cares for my good.

I like the simple definition of a best friend as "a person's closest friend." I also love what business magnate Henry Ford once said: "My best friend brings out the best in me."

Who cares about you more than you do? Think about having a friend who pays attention to the various parts of you. He recognizes the voices that try to protect you when you don't need or want to be protected. The friend names them and sees them for what they are.

Think of this friend hearing that voice saying, "I can't do that," or "What if I fail?" Your best friend calls it out by name, helps you recognize it for what it is, and encourages you to move forward.

Wouldn't that be a great friend, perhaps your best friend? What if such a friend could be with you all the time, helping to bring out the very best in you? Wouldn't you love to have a friend like that?

Well, you already have this friend! It is the part of you that can "see" the best in you. It is the part of you that knows that you are very capable and can do practically anything you set your mind to. It is the part of you that cares and loves you. Your best friend is **you**!

I want to challenge you to become this best friend to yourself. Imagine stifling the negative voices, putting the self-limiting beliefs in their place, and encouraging yourself and doing the things that are in your heart. All you must do is become aware. Let this friend help you. Listen to what he has to say.

The choice is yours. You can become your own best friend, encouraging and inspiring yourself. Or you can continue down the other path of life, not learning to recognize these parts of yourself, listening to the voices that slow you down or stop you dead in your tracks. Which do you prefer?

*"No man is such a conqueror,*
*as the one that has defeated himself."*
— Henry Ward Beecher

To wrap up this chapter, let's apply all of this to reaping.

What happens if you develop these internal parts of yourself so that they are thankful? Imagine being grateful for what you've accomplished, every day.

Stop for a moment and think about an accomplishment in your life. One such accomplishment in my own life was becoming a successful leadership and executive coach before I retired. I am so thankful for how much pleasure and joy this accomplishment added to my life.

I am still reaping benefits from it as I continue to learn and grow, putting this past success to use in ministry work. It has become a part of who I am and fills me with joy as I give to those I walk with. Do I appreciate it? Do I ever! It has become one of my favorite parts of who I am!

Think of an accomplishment that makes you feel this way. It doesn't have to be a major achievement. If you survived a difficult period of life, you have done something great and should be proud.

As you continue to grow in knowing yourself, you will reap rewards. Learn to accept these rewards without condemnation and with joy. Appreciating your achievements will put you on a different path from those who give little or no thought to taking to heart their accomplishments.

I am not saying you should reap in a prideful or selfish way. Just be genuinely thankful for what you accomplish. If it becomes all about you, you're already lost and not very mature at all. But through appreciation of what you've already done, you open the door to achieving so much more.

Reaping is about accumulating with a heart of appreciation, a heart of giving, and a heart of serving others. Appreciating your self can help you live a selfless life, not a selfish one. This is the life that keeps on living.

## CHAPTER SUMMARY

- What you appreciate, appreciates. What you don't appreciate, depreciates.
- Appreciating what you have accomplished will add more value to your life, on which you can build.
- See and name your inner voices to take control of them.
- We all have self-empowering and self-limiting beliefs.
- Your best friend who can encourage and inspire you greatly is you—if you so choose.

**Questions and activities to deepen my learning from this chapter:**

- How can I celebrate a recent accomplishment?
- I will think of a lifelong accomplishment and find a way to celebrate it.
- What steps can I take to become my own best friend?
- What step can I take right now to reap with a heart of appreciation?
- What do I believe about myself? I will work through **Exercises 6 and 7 in Section 3** to find out.

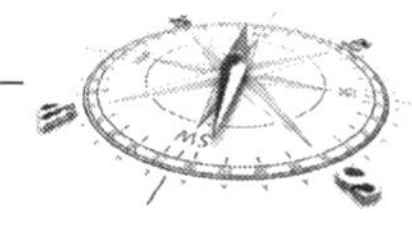

CHAPTER 9

# Bringing It All Together

Let's wrap up with some key concepts. You might have noticed these throughout the book. If not, don't fret, as I will briefly recap them in this final chapter.

## Subject-Object Theory

In the latter part of my life, I have found some truths that have been extremely important to my overall growth. There are a lot of smart people out there studying something called "Constructive Developmental Theory," or simply "Adult Development."

Within Adult Development is something I want to expound on that can literally put you on a path to changing the way you understand things. It's called Subject-Object Theory and can greatly enhance your ability to "see." It's well worth studying.

In a nutshell, when you are subject to something, you are unaware of it. It is such an integral part of you that you are unable to see it. In other words, it is hidden beneath your consciousness.

Sometimes, this can be good. For example, for the most part, we are subject to the process in us that allows us to breathe. That's a good thing, as I most often don't want to have to think about breathing and I prefer it just happen.

However, if there's a part of you that slows your ability to do more in life, that hinders growth, that stops you in your tracks from becoming more of what you are capable of—that's not so good.

When something is object to you, you can see it, think about, and examine it, at least in part. Since you can now "see" it, you can more objectively look at and understand it.

Suddenly, even though it might still be a part of you, you can stand back and reflect and ask questions about it. That's the difference between *subject and object.*

While I just used the example of how we are subject to autonomic processes such as breathing, even *these* can become object. When I run hard, I pay attention to and control my breathing. Sometimes, when I'm under great stress, I will catch myself breathing very shallowly, and I'll correct that by taking a few deep breaths.

When you focus careful attention on your breathing in a mindful way, you can create a great calmness within yourself.

Simply put, when I am *subject* to something, it is in my unconscious and is unseen. When something becomes *object* to me, it is in my conscious mind and can be seen. It goes from being invisible to visible. I move from being blind to it, to becoming enlightened about it.

When I began to swim freestyle, I had to consciously control my breathing. Water in the lungs isn't fun. Eventually, I was able to swim and breathe more automatically, but this did not happen without lots of practice.

The same thing occurs with everything we become conscious about. We learn, over time, to control each thing to the point that they happen mostly automatically.

Think back and look at what we have covered about parts of ourselves/our internal voices, and those self-defeating, self-imposed, self-limiting beliefs. Can you see that they are now becoming object to you?

Perhaps you had never thought about or heard of them before, and in that case, you were completely *subject* to them. Now they have been exposed, so you can identify them and think about them.

You are moving from the position of unawareness to the ability to act on them, rather than *them* doing their act on *you*.

This is how my shift has occurred, and it continues to progress. For years, I did not realize that there were these parts holding me back—yet they greatly affected my behavior, the amount of stress I put on myself, my confidence, and so much more.

It was when my eyes were eventually opened to the concept of parts and internal voices that the transition in me began. For the first time in my life, I began to see things I had no idea even existed.

As I continued to think about my critical inner voices and understand them, I was able to alter the way they controlled me. Literally, many of my thoughts, to which I was once *subject*, became *object* to me.

When something becomes object, you can do something about it. You can reflect, think, question, and act. Will your results change when this happens? You bet!

Overcome just one self-limiting belief and you will begin to create real change in your life. Then do it again and again, as many times as you need. It's the easiest way to change the path you are currently on.

As the old saying goes, "Success begets success." With each success you build, more successes will certainly follow!

## Getting to the Point

As we discussed in Chapter 2, questions—especially powerful questions—can lead to powerful answers. When acted on, these answers can help you realize powerful results.

Since your world is formed by your thoughts, you can enlarge your world by asking yourself powerful, thoughtful questions. The more powerful the questions, the greater the opportunity for real discovery. The greater the discovery, the greater the growth.

As you grow in your mind, your world grows. As your world grows, more opportunities present themselves.

With increased opportunity, you put yourself in a position to reap greater rewards. Greater rewards can lead to a more fulfilling life.

A fulfilled life is a better life and a happier life, with more meaning and with potential for more significance and impact in the world.

Let's look at what is commonly known as the circle of knowledge. Think of what you now know as being contained within the circle shown in Figure 7, your current knowledge capacity. At the edge of the circle you can see something, yet you are not completely aware of what it is. This is "what you know that you don't know," as you only see it in part. Outside of the circle is all the knowledge you don't know and are unaware of, which is as vast as the universe.

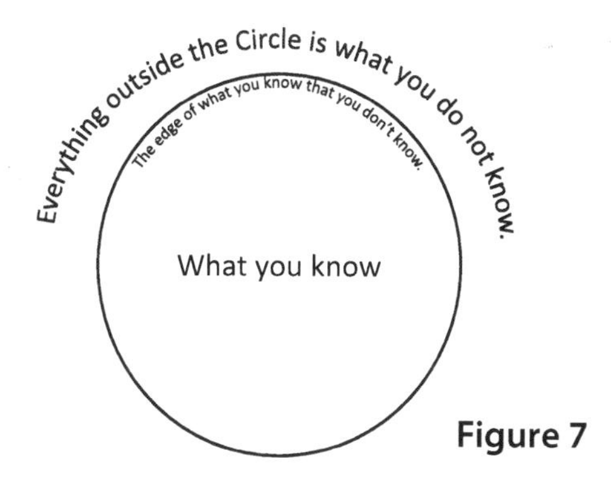


Figure 7

Imagine increasing your knowledge over time. As your circle of knowledge grows, so does the edge of what you know that you don't know, as shown in Figure 8.

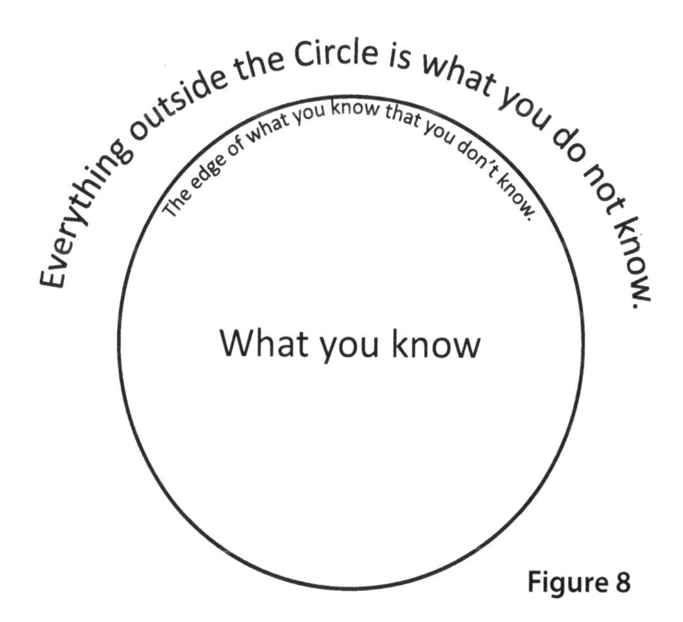


Figure 8

As you continue to gain knowledge, you will find more on the edge of your knowledge, which can stimulate you to continue learning.

Now, instead of letting the circle represent your total knowledge, let it represent what you know about yourself. If you know little about yourself there will be little on the edge of what you know. But as you increase self-awareness, you increase your inner capacity, and the edge of things you know about yourself. This can inspire you to learn more and bring the currently unknown into your realm of understanding.

In Kevin Cashman's book *Leadership from the Inside Out*, there's an old story from pre-revolutionary Russia in which a priest, while walking down a road, is stopped by a soldier.

With his rifle aimed at the priest, the soldier asks, "Who are you? Where are you going? Why are you going there?"

The priest, unfazed by the barrage of questions, replies, "How much do they pay you?"

The surprised soldier responds, "Twenty-five kopeks a month."

The priest pauses and says, in a deeply thoughtful way, "I have a proposal for you. I will pay you fifty kopeks a month if you will stop me every day and challenge me with those same three questions."

1. Who are you?
2. Where are you going?
3. Why are you going there?

I would like to challenge you to try **Exercise 8 in Section 3** entitled "The 30-Day Challenge," which I will also detail here.

During the next month—using your journal, a computer, or just a pen and paper—write down and ask yourself each of the three questions. Be sure to write the date down each time you answer them. Do it for thirty consecutive days. While you might think you will come up with the same answers each day, be forewarned—your answers will change considerably over time.

Each day can add something new, if you seriously consider the questions. At the end of a month, you will have far greater clarity, and greater understanding of yourself, what you really want, and where you are headed.

The process is simple. Write without judgment. This allows what is in your mind to flow naturally and frees up your thinking, eliminating stress. Try to write at the same time each day. For me this was first thing in the morning, but whatever works for you is the right time.

Try ***not*** to look at previous writings. This way, you reduce their influence on what is in your heart each day. Write with enjoyment, without worry, and with a heart of peace to allow you to be more fully present in your writing. Stress and worry close the mind, while fun, lightness, joy, and peace open the mind.

I had days where little surfaced for my answers, and other days where much surfaced. Some days, I had ordinary thoughts, and on other days, the thoughts were extraordinary. Some days I wrote only a few words, yet on other days I would write a great deal.

The insight I gained has been literally invaluable. If you make a legitimate effort at doing this exercise, you will be greatly rewarded. You will have done something that very few people have ever done: taking a look into the deepest parts of your being, unearthing real treasure.

Here's some of what you can expect:

Because your thoughts, moods, and emotions often shift—even if ever so slightly—from one day to the next, you will most likely have some different or new thoughts each day. Again, start fresh without reviewing previous writings, and just try to capture whatever comes to mind.

Second, by asking yourself these three powerful questions repeatedly, you will shift your mind into gear, so to speak. Even your unconscious mind will begin to work on answers and ideas.

Just allow it to happen. Do not strain or stress, or it will close down your thinking. Allow the answers to come naturally. Don't judge your words before you write them down.

You will likely experience a number of real insights, and things will become clearer because of them. You might find new opportunities you have never considered will result.

Third, in getting down to the fundamentals of who you are, where you're going, and why you are going there, you will be taking the leadership position and begin to work *on* your life, rather than just remaining in it.

In other words, you will begin to shift from being *subject* to who you are at present, to moving to the place of making who you are *object*. In this position you can see and examine who you are.

This process might open your mind to seeing things you have never noticed, allowing you to reflect and question them, to develop new perspectives. Your thinking will automatically be enlarged and will allow you to become more of who you really want to be.

On this last point, some of the most impactful questions ever posed to me came from Jim Rohn, once known as America's foremost business philosopher. I remember this time in my life well. It was back in the early 1980s. As I drove down the highway, I listened to one of Jim's many cassette tape series.

He said:

> "We can have more than we've got because we can **become** more than we are."

And he stated simply:

> "The most important question to ask on the job is not 'What am I getting?'
>
> The most important question to ask on the job is **'What am I becoming?'**"

The question "What am I becoming?" is about you and where you are going. It is about how you are growing. It shows you what is truly important to you, and what is not important to you. It helps you see who you are now and who you want to be. This question is about the outcome of your life. It's working on it, not just in it.

To not ask this last question robs you of awareness regarding what is happening in your life. In other words, if you don't think about it, life will just happen to you. Instead, you can make decisions and take actions to create the life you want.

So get serious and ask yourself, "What am I becoming?" The previous exercise will help you clarify this very important question. Your life, your happiness, and your significance are good reasons not to skip the exercise.

Is your life worth working on? Something else Jim admonished was to "work harder on yourself than you do on your job." Success on the job, and in any part of our lives, comes more from who we are and who we're becoming than anything else.

Going beyond success to true significance requires that you know who you truly are. It's out of you, who you are, that you get what you get.

Work on yourself. Invest in yourself. You are a very important investment, after all. Become more than you are now and continue this practice throughout your life. The results can be beyond anything you can imagine.

Are you worth it? You bet.

What's your next move?

After doing the 30-Day exercise, write the answer to the question "What am I becoming?" Put down the first thing that comes to mind. Then review it, restate it, and continue until you are crystal clear.

Once you are clear, mark your calendar to review what you have written in a few days. See what else comes up. It's your life. Your life has incalculable value.

Putting forth a little effort now can give you a life that ends with a great deal more satisfaction and far less regret. You will never regret working *on* your life, instead of just in it.

## Personal Vision

*"We become what we dream."*
*— Richard Boyatzis*

We've saved the best and most important exercise for last. Why? If you have worked through this book and have done the exercises up to this point, you will have far more clarity than when you began. Now you are ready to cast your personal vision.

What is vision? It's seeing life in a way that is meaningful to you, that is your dream of what your life will look like and how it will end. Vision consists of who you are, what you do, what you are becoming, and who you'll ultimately be.

Vision helps you cast a dream of your ideal life. When you have a vision for your life, you can align what you do with what you ultimately need and want. You can create a pathway to the future, creating what you envision.

To quote some wisdom from one of the oldest translations of Scripture: "Where there is no vision, the people perish" (Proverbs 29:18).

If you don't have a vision for your life, what roadmap are you following? You might as well shoot an arrow into the air with no target in sight. Just be careful you are not standing directly under it! You need to create a vision for your life so you'll have something to aim for.

As you live your life, your vision will be widened or narrowed. Since it is your personal vision, you are free to clarify it as you move through life. I recommend revisiting your vision at the beginning of each year, to continue to validate and adjust it as needed. Imagine the potential of fulfilling your vision if you do this. What a life you can create!

I recommend you stop now and complete **Exercise 9, entitled "Personal Vision," in Section 3.**

A few final things about your vision. The length of your vision is not important, but the clarity of it is. The more *clearly* you can see it, the more likely it will happen.

Who should you share your vision with? As we have said before, "Life is relationship," so it's important to share your vision with someone close to you. Choose someone who will help you become accountable to working toward your vision. They may even be a part of helping you fulfill it.

Imagine having someone that believes in you and who is willing to invest in your vision. A major truth stated in Scripture is, "And if one prevail against him, two shall withstand him; and a threefold cord is not quickly broken" (Ecclesiastes 4:12).

There is strength in relationship that will help you succeed. Choose those you wish to share your life and vision with, and then do it! Don't forget to help them find and fulfill their vision as well. The reward to each of you will be great.

## What's the Bottom Line?

Here's the bottom line of this book. Your thoughts make up your life. They make you who you are and who you are becoming.

The question is, who do you want to become? It's your choice. If you follow the path laid out in this book, you might see things you had not previously seen.

You might think things you had not previously thought, which will give you more to choose from and can move you to do new things, which will create completely new results.

If you start upon this path, you will become the major creative force in your life, rather than allowing other things and people to create your life for you.

As we close out this chapter, let's look at some truths about results, the ultimate goal of using the S.T.A.R. Approach in your life. While this list is long, soon you'll be able to add many items of your own.

The truth about results. Results happen:

- From what I do, not just from what I know.
- From who I am, and who I'm becoming.
- From what I feed with time, attention, and resources.
- When I live intentionally and creatively, rather than reactively or responsively.
- From clarifying my values, which affect my priorities.
- When I'm ready to get unstuck from the old, familiar ways.

- When I get rid of self-imposed limitations and self-limiting beliefs.
- Because of the time and attention I give to what really matters.
- When I take risks to create what I want.
- When I move from self-protection to self-actualization.
- From self-energizing, self-empowering beliefs.
- When I embrace my fears, rather than allowing them to embrace me.
- When I move from subject to object.
- As a part of my relationships—always.
- When I encourage the best in others.
- From exploring more perspectives.
- From seeing more possibilities.
- In the being, from which comes the doing.
- To enrich my life and the lives of those around you.
- To expand my life.
- To increase the significance of my life.

Remember, results happen when you take control of your life, actively creating it, not from just allowing life to happen to you. Results come from working *on* your life, not just *in* it. Take control of the reins and guide your life in a better direction. Create the *you* that creates a different life.

Now that you know how the S.T.A.R. Approach can guide you from passing through life to taking charge of it, I leave you with these questions. The answers will determine the course of your future:

Who do you want to become?

What do you want to have accomplished in the end?

What will you do now?

## CHAPTER SUMMARY

- You are subject to some thoughts, things, people, and situations—see them and make them object to you.
- You can turn something you are subject to into a manageable object by thinking it through.
- Pay attention to the edge of knowing: what you know that you don't yet know. That's where learning takes place.
- Remember the Russian soldier's three questions.

**Questions and activities to deepen my learning from this chapter:**

- What can I move from subject to object? In other words, what is hidden that is controlling my life, and how can I make it known?
- What can I do to increase my circle of knowledge, to increase what I know that I don't know? How will I know if it's working?
- I will take the 30-Day challenge. Commit to the exercise for a few minutes daily for the full thirty days, and notice how my answers evolve. When I finish the thirty days, I will answer the final three questions in this chapter.

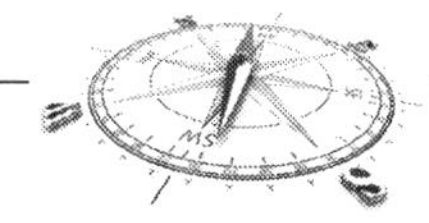

# Afterword

I hope you take away more from this book than only my thoughts and experience.

My dream for this book is to help others begin their own journeys of self-discovery and enlightenment, which they can share with others.

My dream is to help others grow their intelligence in a different way—not just the cognitive variety of knowledge that most equate to intelligence, but in the many other dimensions of intelligence—the intelligence in their emotions, in maturity, and in relationships, I want to help people grow in their natural strengths, in wisdom, spiritually, and in the many other types of intelligence available to each of us.

I also want to help you see into and *predict your future* by setting your course and following through. As Peter Drucker once admonished: "The best way to predict your future is to create it."

Now, before you think this is some strange gobbledygook, let me explain what I mean. Can you actually predict the future? Yes, we all can to a degree.

What do I mean? Well, whenever we do something, by taking action, something happens or is created in the future. Sometimes it's what we expect, sometimes not. The further away it is, time-wise, the less accurate our prediction might be. This requires us to regularly check our course and make corrections as needed.

What if you don't take action? You can predict the result.

What if you do take action, but don't monitor the result? It's still possible to predict the result.

But what if you take action and **do** monitor the result? What do you think might happen?

What if you notice the result is potentially different than what you intended? Unless you see it, reflect on what to do, and take another action to affect its course, what will result?

Yes, we can predict the future outcome of many of our actions. For example, if you save consistently, accumulate more, and have more available to you in the future, you can predict a comfortable retirement.

If you get in the car, drive to the store, buy a half-gallon of ice cream, and return home, I bet I can predict the future—there is a high probability you will eventually eat some of the ice cream. I sure would!

What if you come home with the "result" and fail to take the next step by putting the ice cream in the freezer? While not every result requires more action, many do. If you pay no attention to it, don't check your course, or avoid taking the necessary action, what will the result be? It's worth paying attention to keep the ice cream from melting, isn't it?

While this last scenario of going to the store may seem simplistic on the surface, it contains a truth. Every action is premeditated. You determined in your mind you wanted some ice cream, so you created the necessary steps to get it. Did I just say created? Yes, exactly.

Whenever we want something, even something as simple as ice cream—or as complex as a retirement fund, or a painting, or a home—we create each step along the way. Our clarity about what we want and our desire to get it determine what we do, which leads to creating the steps required to obtain whatever it is.

It can be the creation itself, in the case of a painting. Isn't this true of the retirement account? It becomes something you created. While the ice cream may be something someone else created, you created the desire for it, and you fulfilled the desire. It became yours with the money you earned. Your work created the receipt of the money needed to purchase it.

Everything in life, literally, is somehow connected with creating. Everything. You can choose to take the actions needed to create whatever it is you want, or you can allow your reactions or your responses to others and other things to create whatever it is.

Better that you are in charge of the creating, isn't it?

We go after things we want, whether someone else created them or we create them, and we create the path to get there. Even when we don't consciously think about it, the next step is decided on or created, and it moves us closer to what we want.

So here's my final question for you:

**What kind of life do you want to create?**

## Section 3

# Exercises and Resources

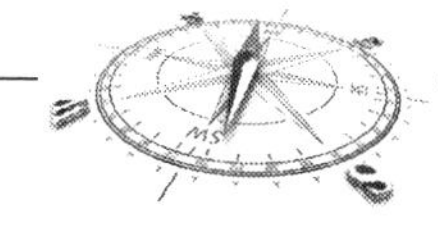

EXERCISE 1

# Developing Greater Perspective

During this exercise, you will attempt to uncover as many points of view as possible. It is always helpful to have someone ask you the questions, and where appropriate, to follow up with the question "and what else?" An outline of the exercise is as follows:

- Choosing a topic and current viewpoint/perspective
- Developing multiple viewpoints/perspectives
    - Attempt to choose up to eight or more alternative viewpoints.
- Examining possible actions
    - Choose as many possible actions as you can develop.
- Choosing the most important action you can take.
- Instilling accountability.

A Viewpoint/Perspective form follows this page. Before using this exercise, I suggest you read through the sample exercise with John, an actual person (his name was changed) on the following pages for insight into how to use it with yourself or in helping someone else.

## Viewpoint/Perspective Form

Topic: ______________________________

Current Viewpoint/Perspective:

______________________________

______________________________

Generate up to eight or more alternative viewpoints:

1. ______________________________
2. ______________________________
3. ______________________________
4. ______________________________
5. ______________________________
6. ______________________________
7. ______________________________
8. ______________________________

Generate as many potential action steps as you can:

1. ______________________________
2. ______________________________
3. ______________________________
4. ______________________________
5. ______________________________
6. ______________________________

— continued on next page —

Choose an action or actions to execute:

How can you hold yourself accountable?

## Sample Exercise

The topic and John's current viewpoint were chosen as follows:

**Topic**: Saving for retirement

**Current viewpoint**: I have plenty of time ahead to plan and am making regular contributions to my savings and 401K.

As we begin examining alternative viewpoints, I encourage John to not only look at pragmatic, logical things, but to also use his intuition, desires, emotions, what other people may think, and anything else that serves in developing a holistic understanding of the possibilities he has. We start by asking "What other viewpoints are there?"

Our target is to generate at least five to eight alternative viewpoints. To continue uncovering new viewpoints requires asking "and what else?" several times.

**Alternative viewpoint #1**: While I have some money saved, and continue to save, I'm not sure if I am saving enough.

**Alternative viewpoint #2**: I'm still young and have plenty of time to plan and decide, yet I have this strong feeling inside I need to do something.

**Alternative viewpoint #3**: I have responsibility for my family and should consider them in what I am doing.

**Alternative viewpoint #4**: I could max out my 401K and take better advantage of the tax savings and company match.

**Alternative viewpoint #5**: I could stop adding to the 401K and have more money to pay off the house and cars to get out of debt.

**Alternative viewpoint #6**: I could work with someone, maybe a financial manager, to check what I am doing and develop a plan that might serve me better now and later.

**Alternative viewpoint #7**: I can consider what would happen if I lost my job at some point and couldn't save anything.

**Alternative viewpoint #8**: I wonder what my wife thinks about our savings? We have not discussed it.

Satisfied with what he had at this point, John began to explore what actions would be best for him to take and came up with the following:

**Potential action #1**: Not worry about it now and look into it later.

**Potential action #2**: Stop the withdrawals for the 401K and pay down my debt.

**Potential action #3**: Get with HR about my 401K plan so I can better understand what options I have available to me.

**Potential action #4:** Meet with a financial manager and develop a plan.

**Potential action #5:** Speak with my wife and make the decisions with her on what to do next.

Satisfied with these possible actions, John is now at a point the point where he decides to make a choice that will best serve his values, needs, and desires.

**Action:** I think it is important that I discuss this with my wife, meet with HR to better understand my company's 401K plan, and find someone that can help us do some financial planning.

The final step is to build in some accountability. I asked John, "How can you hold yourself accountable to take these actions?"

> **Accountability #1**: I will speak with my wife tonight, and believe me, she will keep me accountable! This really is too important, after all.

I then asked, "And what else?"

> **Accountability #2**: I am putting on my calendar to speak with our HR person tomorrow morning, and to find someone to help me with a plan.

For some topics one point of accountability will be sufficient, while for others, several may be needed. The stronger the accountability, the more likely action will be taken and results will be gained.

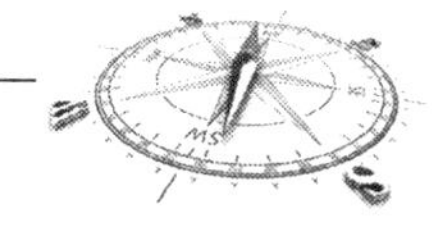

EXERCISE 2

# Cycles/Patterns

Think about something in your life that seems to happen again and again, that you want to improve. Maybe it's something you do in your job, or the way you treat your wife or kids at a certain time. Perhaps it's how you use your weekends or your downtime. It could also be something physical, such as how you play basketball, your golf swing, or any sport or activity. It could be playing a musical instrument, how you carry a tune in choir, you name it. Once you have the activity, answer the following questions:

*S*ee it more clearly: What do I notice about it?

Ask "and what else" at least three times:

*T*hink about it more deeply: What can I do to change or improve it?

Ask "and what else" at least three times:

*A*ct in a way to make a change: What can I do to make it happen?

Ask "and what else" at least three times:

What one action will you firmly commit to now?

*R*eap a new result: How will I know when I am there? Describe the result in detail.

And what else?

You will find a form and sample for this exercise on the following pages.

## Cycles/Patterns Form

See it more clearly: What do I notice about it?

________________________________________

________________________________________

Ask "and what else" at least three times:

1. ____________________________________
2. ____________________________________
3. ____________________________________

Think about it more deeply: What can I do to change or improve it?

________________________________________

________________________________________

Ask "and what else" at least three times:

1. ____________________________________
2. ____________________________________
3. ____________________________________

Act in a way to make a change: What can I do to make it happen? Start each answer with "I will."

________________________________________

________________________________________

________________________________________

________________________________________

— continued on next page —

Ask "and what else" at least three times:

1.________________________________________

2.________________________________________

3.________________________________________

What one action will you firmly commit to now?

____________________________________________

____________________________________________

*R*eap a new result: How will I know when I am there? Describe the result in detail.

____________________________________________

____________________________________________

____________________________________________

____________________________________________

And what else?

____________________________________________

____________________________________________

____________________________________________

____________________________________________

An example of this exercise is on the following page.

## Sample Exercise

See it more clearly: What do I notice about it?

Every day when I get home from work, I tend to be impatient and short-tempered with my wife.

Ask "and what else" at least three times:

1. I'm tired from working all day and the long drive home.
2. I've spent my energy all day going from one project to another and in meetings.
3. I just want some downtime to unwind at the end of the day.

Think about it more deeply: What can I do to change or improve it? Start each answer with "I can."

I can change my attitude toward my wife when I get home, if I really want to.

Ask "and what else" at least three times:

1. I can change the way I always rush to get home, purposely slow down and not get so frustrated at the traffic. After all, it's not going to change anytime soon.
2. I can learn to leave my job at the office by spending a few minutes at the end of each day writing down what I did not finish and what I want to accomplish the next day.
3. I can sit in the car a few minutes to unwind before going inside my house.
4. I can renew my appreciation for my wife and family. I can begin to be thankful for them.

*A*ct in a way to make a change: What can I do to make it happen? Start each answer with "I will."

I will begin implementing the idea on taking a few minutes at the end of the day to note what was left undone and put it on my calendar for the next day.

Ask "and what else" at least three times:

1. I will work on keeping my temper under control on my drive home, because I can't change the traffic or other drivers, I can only control myself. I will put on some music and try to lighten up.
2. I will think about the blessing my wife is to me, how empty my life would be without her, and how full it is with her.
3. I will not go into the house until I feel calm inside.

What one action will you firmly commit to now?

I will immediately start clearing my mind from work by working on my calendar for the next day.

*R*eap a new result: How will I know when I am there? Describe the result in detail.

When I have the result of more calmness and peace in my life more often, I will have succeeded. It will feel great and I will become less burdened as I reap the results from my efforts.

What else?

My life can change from being so hurried all the time to enjoying my life more, especially with the most important person in the world to me. I can use this change to affect other things in my life such as learning how to unwind and relax more often during each day.

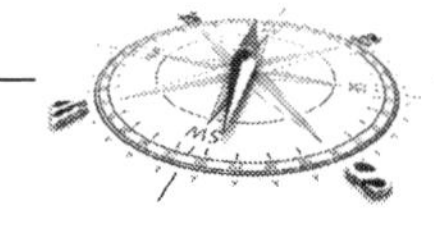

EXERCISE 3

# Personal Values

Following is a quick exercise to get you started on understanding your values. Review the list of values below and check or circle ones that are important to you. Note that, while the following list contains a good number of values, there are a few blank boxes at the end of the list where you can add values that might not be listed.

Next, narrow the list down and rank order the top five. There are no right or wrong answers; choose those that seem most true to what you hold most valuable, and not what you think someone else would say.

This exercise will allow you to better understand yourself. With greater awareness comes the ability to make better, more deliberate decisions that align with who you are.

| Personal Values |
|---|
| **Achievement** – accomplishment; mastery; achieving goals |
| **Action** – fast-paced, high activity |
| **Advancement** – moving up in my organization or my profession |
| **Adventure** – new and challenging opportunities; excitement; risk |
| **Aesthetics** – appreciating and creating beauty around me |

| Personal Values |
|---|
| **Affiliation** – interacting with others; belonging |
| **Affluence** – high income; financial success; prosperity |
| **Authority** – position and power to control events and others' activities |
| **Balance** – a lifestyle that allows for work, family, self, community |
| **Challenge** – taking on complex, demanding tasks and responsibilities |
| **Change** – being without a routine; frequent changes in responsibility or venue; unpredictability and spontaneity |
| **Collaboration** – close, cooperative relationships with others |
| **Community** – serving a purpose that supersedes personal desires |
| **Competency** – demonstrating high proficiency and knowledge; showing above-average effectiveness |
| **Competition** – rivalry, with winning as the goal |
| **Connection** – relating deeply with others |
| **Courage** – standing up for my beliefs and/or taking daring action |
| **Creativity** – discovering or developing new ideas or things; imagination |
| **Curiosity** – natural inclination to explore, ask questions, probe, and understand |
| **Duty** – respect for authority, rules, and regulations |
| **Economic security** – steady and secure employment; being conservative in my approach to risk |
| **Enjoyment** – fun, laughter, joy |

| Personal Values |
|---|
| **Excellence** – doing things in an above-average manner; stretching to be your best |
| **Experimentation** – trying new and different ways, perhaps just to see what happens |
| **Fame** – prominence; being well known |
| **Fitness** – health, physical and mental well-being; vitality; staying in shape |
| **Frugality** – keeping spending reined in; saving money; reusing items |
| **Harmony** – keeping and restoring peace among people; being a peacemaker |
| **Humor/lightness** – laughing at myself, laughing at life |
| **Independence** – acting autonomously with few constraints; being self-sufficient and self-reliant; able to act on my own. |
| **Influence** – having an impact on others; persuasiveness |
| **Inner harmony** – contentment; being at peace with self |
| **Innovating** – creating something new |
| **Integrity** – acting in accordance with ethical and moral standards; honesty |
| **Intimacy** – close personal relationships; love and affection |
| **Justice** – fairness; equality; doing the right thing |
| **Leadership** – stepping into leadership opportunities and roles |
| **Learning** – gaining new knowledge, perspective, insight, information, understanding, skill |
| **Location** – choice of place to live |
| **Loyalty** – being faithful; dedication to individuals, organizations, or traditions |

| Personal Values |
| --- |
| **Openness** – being open to others; vulnerable |
| **Order** – stability; organization; lack of chaos |
| **Nature** – experiencing and being in nature |
| **Personal growth** – maximizing my potential; developing and learning; increasing my self-knowledge |
| **Play** – integrating play into relationships; laughter and fun; sports |
| **Power** – being powerful; coming from your own strengths; exerting power |
| **Precision** – finding and creating precise, specific answers |
| **Questioning** – probing deeper; inquiry |
| **Recognition** – positive feedback and public credit for accomplishments |
| **Reflection** – taking time to ponder |
| **Responsibility** – dependability; reliability; accountability for results |
| **Self-reliance** – acting from my own means |
| **Service** – helping others attain their goals; providing care and support |
| **Simplicity** – designing my life without an excess of physical objects or commitments |
| **Solitude** – creating time to be alone |
| **Spirituality** – strong spiritual or religious beliefs |
| **Status** – being respected for one's job or position or association |
| **Unique** – being quirky; dressing or acting in an unconventional or unusual way |

Of the values you marked, write the five most important to you at this time below:

1. ______________________________
2. ______________________________
3. ______________________________
4. ______________________________
5. ______________________________

If forced to compromise on any of these five, which one would it be? ____________

Which of the five would you be most reluctant to give up? _______

For each of your top five values, concisely describe what it means to you. In other words, what is your definition of that value? How does it impact you in your personal and work/professional life?

Value 1: ______________________________

______________________________

______________________________

______________________________

Value 2: ______________________________

______________________________

______________________________

______________________________

— continued on next page —

Value 3: ______________________________

______________________________

______________________________

______________________________

Value 4: ______________________________

______________________________

______________________________

______________________________

Value 5: ______________________________

______________________________

______________________________

______________________________

What do you notice about your values?

What takeaways do you have now that you have examined your values?

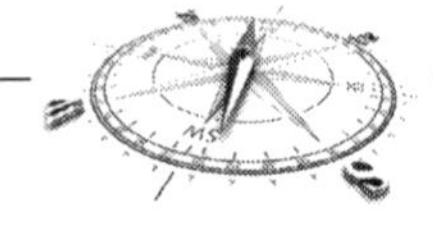

EXERCISE 4

# Needs

Here's a key to living a more meaningful and fulfilled life: Let what you *must have* take precedence over what you *want*. Or put another way, live to your needs, not your desires. If you want to further differentiate wants and needs, review the section in Chapter Five, entitled "Do You Want It, or Need It?"

Give some thought to what you really need to have a meaningful and fulfilling life. What is most important to you? Which things would you put yourself in harm's way for, or even die for? Without them you would experience a great deal of stress.

Remember: These things come from being selfless, not selfish. They are tied to who you are and your very identity. They are outward-focused.

For example, some of my needs include:

1. My faith
2. Good relationships with my wife, close family, and close friends
3. Being a good provider for my family
4. Meaningful work that helps others improve their lives
5. To spend my time wisely

— continued on next page —

List at least five of your deep needs below:

1. ______________________________
2. ______________________________
3. ______________________________
4. ______________________________
5. ______________________________

What do I notice about these needs?

What steps will I take today toward fulfilling these needs?

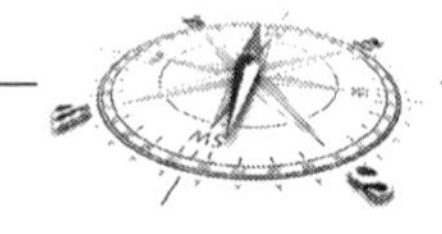

EXERCISE 5

# Prioritizing

The following forms are self-explanatory. I recommend starting with things that tend to consume most of your time and energy. Once you have identified where your time goes, you can begin to make decisions about which actions to take.

You can use the previous exercises to develop a broader perspective on what is important, allowing you to make the best decisions possible. The advantage of using this system is, it can help you see where you can focus your time and reduce stress, provided you take action in the top quadrants.

I recommend re-reading the beginning of Chapter 6 to gain the greatest benefit from this exercise. While the Urgent and Important quadrant speaks for itself, an important thing to note is the Important but Not Urgent quadrant. This quadrant is critical to creating more of what you want in the future. Spend as much time as is reasonable doing the items in this category.

To further enhance your productivity, eliminate or avoid as many of the items in the bottom two quadrants. Most are truly time-wasters and can consume an enormous part of your life in a very unproductive manner.

Once you've identified your Important and Urgent items, as well as your Important but Not Urgent items, you can create a to-do list that, once accomplished, can move you forward.

The Priority Matrix form on the next page is followed by a guide to completing the form.

# Priority Matrix Guide

| | Urgent | Not Urgent |
|---|---|---|
| **Important** | **Manage** (Necessity) — Imp. & Urgent — Responding | **Focus** (Quality and Personal Leadership) — Imp. But Not Urgent — Creating |
| | Crises | Preparation |
| | Medical emergencies | Planning & strategizing |
| | Other true emergencies | Relationship-building |
| | Pressing problems | Exercise |
| | Last-minute preparations | True recreation/relaxation |
| | Deadlines that must be met now | Empowerment |
| **Not Important** | **Avoid** (Deception) — Not Imp. But Urgent — Reacting | **Eliminate** (Waste) — Not Imp. & Not Urgent — Reacting |
| | Interruptions | Trivial busywork |
| | Some phone calls | Some emails |
| | Some meetings | Calls that can be handled by others |
| | Many pressing matters | Time wasters |
| | Many popular activities | Escape activities |
| | Others' priorities or expectations | Mindless TV, internet surfing |

## Priority Matrix

| | Urgent | Not Urgent |
|---|---|---|
| Important | Imp. & Urgent — **Manage** (Necessity) — Responding | Imp. But Not Urgent — **Focus** (Quality and Personal Leadership) — Creating |
| Not Important | Not Imp. But Urgent — **Avoid** (Deception) — Reacting | Not Imp. & Not Urgent — **Avoid** (Waste) — Reacting |

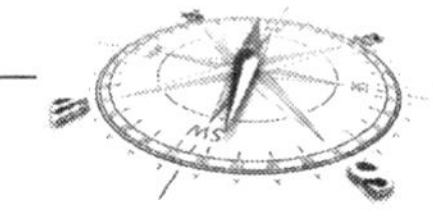

EXERCISE 6

# Self-Empowering Beliefs

Think of some things you do well. List as many as you can and ask yourself the questions shown below.

The objective of this exercise is to take things which are somewhat hidden to you, that you may be subject to, and to bring them out—literally, to make them into an object you can examine and explore.

On the form following this page, you will find the questions. The first question asks what you are good at. There is a part of you that just knows you are good at these things. You may even hear yourself saying, "I am really good at _________."

The remaining questions help you examine, and hopefully experience, the satisfaction of each belief.

Repeat this exercise in your journal, listing *at least ten items or more* for things you believe you are good at. Remember, this is what *you* believe about yourself, not what someone else believes, so disregard anything that comes to mind telling you it isn't true. Write down what is true to you, in your mind and heart.

To repeat this exercise ten times can take a bit of work, but it will lead you to self-discovery beyond anything you have previously known or thought.

Two examples follow the form on the next page.

## Self-Empowering Belief Form

First Question: What is something I am good at or confident in?

Answer:________________________________________

______________________________________________

Second Question: What does this make me think and believe about myself?

Answer:________________________________________

______________________________________________

______________________________________________

______________________________________________

Third Question: What's important about this?

Answer:________________________________________

______________________________________________

______________________________________________

______________________________________________

What do I notice about what I believe of myself?

__________________________________________________

__________________________________________________

__________________________________________________

__________________________________________________

__________________________________________________

__________________________________________________

How can I leverage these things in my life?

## Example A

First Question: What is something I am good at or confident in?

Answer: I am good at learning new things, especially about myself. I love to read books on how the mind works.

Second Question: What does this make me think and believe about myself?

Answer: I really enjoy learning, as it makes me feel like I'm accomplishing something in my life. The more I learn about myself, the more confident I am about my growth and the future.

Third Question: What's important about this?

Answer: I believe I'm not only capable of learning, but that I am learning and growing. Continuing to learn has helped me achieve a lot during my life, giving me a real strength as I continue to grow and develop my mind. I'm good at it and want to continue it throughout my life.

What do I notice about what I believe of myself?

I have a strong learning and growth mindset and can learn anything I put my mind to. The world is my oyster!

How can I leverage these things in my life?

I can write and teach more, each of which is very satisfying to me. I can continue to sit at the feet of those who have gone before me, which I love to do through reading their books. I can keep my brain healthy through exercise and learning.

## Example B

First Question: What is something I am good at or confident in?

Answer: Playing the guitar.

Second Question: What does this make me think and believe about myself?

Answer: Playing the guitar makes me feel good. Playing older songs takes me back to some great times when I was young. Learning new songs can be challenging at times but is so rewarding to me. It makes me happy and thankful I can still play.

Third Question: What's important about this?

Answer: It's a great way for me to relax. I believe I can play virtually anything, given time and practice. I can always improve but I'm better than average and will continue enjoying it as often as I can.

What do I notice about what I believe of myself?

I love music and have always had an ear for it. While I don't plan on playing in a band again, it does give me joy in my life.

How can I leverage these things in my life?

Playing the guitar and listening to music is an important part of my life which I will continue to enjoy for the rest of my life. I will take great pleasure by continuing to listen to the good old tunes and learning new ones!

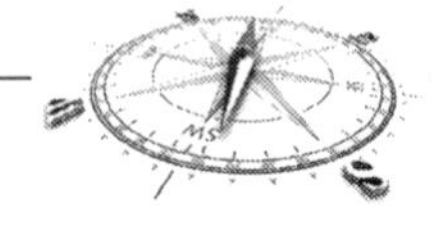

EXERCISE 7

# Self-Limiting Beliefs

Let's look at some self-limiting beliefs. If you do this exercise, you will not regret it. I have yet to see a single person who has done the exercise not come away with a keener sense of themselves and find areas in which they can change for the better.

If you complete this exercise with an open mind, you'll see things you may never have realized existed.

Find a nice, comfortable place without distractions and notice any tension in your body. Notice any tightness around your forehead, around your eyes. Release it. Notice any stress elsewhere in your face. Let go of the tension. Notice any stress elsewhere in your body, such as in your neck and shoulders. Relax. Release the tension. Take a few slow, deep breaths, exhaling slowly each time. When you feel relaxed, begin the exercise.

Think of some things you tell yourself that you do *not* do well and list as many as you can. As with the previous exercise, the objective here is to make things visible that you may not otherwise see, that you are subject to. The exercise will help you make them separate, into objects you can examine and explore.

The first question asks about what you tell yourself you don't believe you are good at, or something you fear. Everyone has experienced this, so with a little self-reflection, you will likely find several.

We're not talking about things that might be impossible, such as running a four-minute mile—although some of you might be able to do that! No, this is something you might be able to do, or would like to be able to do, yet have some doubts about.

You might even experience this as a voice in your head that says, "I not good at __________."

The second question is about noticing your emotions and the feelings in your body.

The third question asks you to look at what you tell yourself in your mind as you examine this belief. Then you will dispute the answer.

Ask yourself the truth about it and answer the final questions to make a choice to move forward and take action.

Notice the pattern of *seeing, thinking, and acting* to position yourself to *reap* something new once again.

I recommend you repeat this exercise in your journal for at least ten things you believe you are not good at.

On the following pages, I will share some self-limiting beliefs I worked through in my life. Fortunately, each of these examples was overcome completely—but it took me considerable time and effort to do so.

Unfortunately, the unveiling of this self-sabotage was a slow process for me. I had no one to help me open it up in the way that I now understand it. This is one of the reasons I developed this exercise—so you don't have to learn it the way I did. Now you have a process that can save considerable time. If it doesn't work best for you in the way I have laid it out, modify it so it works for you.

You can add one additional step that can make the results even more impactful. Work through your self-limiting beliefs with someone you trust, perhaps even a coach. Don't ask them to try to "fix" you or to provide solutions to you until you have exhausted your own effort on each of the questions.

It can help tremendously to have someone listen to what you have to say and then challenge you to act. Or perhaps they will encourage you or provide examples from their own life to help you think more deeply. Involving someone else also tends to make you more accountable to get it done.

Remember, this is what you believe about yourself, not what someone else says, so disregard outside influences as much as you can—just write down what comes to mind about yourself.

## Self-Limiting Belief Form

First Question: What is something I don't believe I'm good at or something I fear?

Answer:________________________________________

________________________________________________

Second Question: How does it make me feel emotionally or in my body and thoughts?

Answer:________________________________________

________________________________________________

________________________________________________

What can I name this part of me?

Answer:________________________________________

Third Question: What do I believe about this? What am I telling myself?

Answer:________________________________________

________________________________________________

________________________________________________

________________________________________________

Dispute the Answer: _______________________________

________________________________________________

________________________________________________

________________________________________________

Fourth Question: What do I want to do about this?

Answer:___________________________________________

___________________________________________

___________________________________________

___________________________________________

On a scale of 1 to 10, with 10 being absolutely committed to doing this, where am I? __________

What can I do to move it closer to a 10? ____________

Answer:___________________________________________

___________________________________________

___________________________________________

___________________________________________

___________________________________________

___________________________________________

___________________________________________

How can I hold myself accountable for doing the work needed to accomplish this?

Answer:___________________________________________

___________________________________________

___________________________________________

___________________________________________

___________________________________________

___________________________________________

## Example A

First Question: What is something I don't believe I'm good at or something I fear?

Answer: I am not very good at speaking in front of a group.

Second Question: How does it make me feel emotionally or in my body and thoughts?

Answer: It makes me so nervous, I literally shake. I panic. My stomach gets tied up in knots. I can't think and I wind up at a complete loss for words. I freeze.

What can I name this part of me?

Answer: Frozen Bill!

Third Question: What do I believe about this? What am I telling myself?

Answer: That I can't do it, so why even put myself into a situation where I might have to. I don't know that I could ever be comfortable with public speaking. Ever. I just have so much doubt I could even do it.

Dispute the answer: This just isn't true. I can speak with one, two, or even a few people just fine. I can learn how, and I can develop the skill if I will just spend time doing so. Even though I have been nervous speaking in some situations, I'm not always terrified, especially when I really know my subject. I can speak to others in a small group when they are family or friends. It is a lie that to say I can't do this. I just need to learn how.

Fourth Question: What do I want to do about this?

Answer: I want to change it. I want to learn and gain confidence in my ability to speak to a group.

On a scale of 1 to 10, with 10 being absolutely committed to doing this, where am I? *8*

What can you do to move it closer to a 10?

Answer: Considering I need to be able to do this if I ever want to be promoted, which I do, I will make it happen. I can take some public speaking classes at the local community center and will sign up immediately. I will find a good book or two on the subject and will purchase them today. I've even heard about Toastmasters. I'll check into that and see what it's about. I will put myself out there at work, jump off the cliff, and see what happens.

How can I hold myself accountable for doing the work needed to accomplish these things?

Answer: I will talk with my wife this evening and to my boss today to see if the company can provide some help. I'll let them both know I want and need their help to keep me accountable to making this happen.

## Example B

First Question: What is something I don't believe I'm good at or something I fear?

Answer: I'm afraid to leave this job.

Second Question: How does it make me feel emotionally or in my body and thoughts?

Answer: Like I will fail and be seen as a failure. I worry about how I would be able to take care of my family. The thought is scary to me. The thought of not providing for my family almost makes me feel sick on my stomach.

What can I name this part of me?

Answer: Fearful Bill!

Third Question: What do I believe about this? What am I telling myself?

Answer: I'm better off just doing my job and toughing it out. Even if I found a new job, how do I know it will be any better? What if I wind up back in the same situation?

Dispute the answer: Why does this have to be true? Yes, I may be afraid, but who says I can't find a better job, or do more in the one I have now? Even if I failed, there are more jobs out there. If I don't look, how will I even know? And I can keep this job until I find something.

Fourth Question: What do I want to do about this?

Answer: I want to have a better job with more responsibility, more opportunity for advancement, and more income with great benefits. I want to advance in my career and not feel so stuck.

On a scale of 1 to 10, with 10 being absolutely committed to doing this, where am I? 9

What can you do to move it closer to a 10?

> Answer: I'm going to speak with my wife and think it through more this evening. In fact, I will sharpen up my resume immediately and quietly being looking for another job. I will have a discussion with my good friend John to get his take on it, since he's done it before. I will also speak with HR and see if there may be other opportunities in the company for me before the week is out.

How can I hold myself accountable for doing the work needed to accomplish this?

> Answer: My wife will hold me accountable once I tell her, I'm sure of that! I know John really well, too, and I'm sure he will help me stay on track. I will also put some dates for finishing my resume update and speaking to John on my calendar right now.

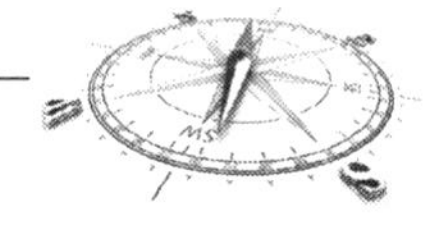

EXERCISE 8

# The 30-Day Challenge

Who? Where? Why?

How would you like to do something simple that is guaranteed to change how you see your life? It will add more clarity and understanding to who you are, where you're going, and the reason you're going there.

This is based on the story in Chapter 9 under "Getting to the Point." I challenge you to take the next thirty days and answer the following three questions in your journal.

Some time ago I created a document on my computer titled "My 30-Day Challenge" to allow me to continue to have easy access to what I wrote and add to it over time.

You will be amazed at the result if you take this challenge. This exercise can literally change your life.

The format is simple:

Date and the day number (June 1, Day 1, etc.)

1. Who am I?
2. Where am I going?
3. Why am I going there?

A few items to note as you write each day:

1. Try to write without judgment as much as possible—neither your own judgment, nor anyone else's.

2. Do not look at previous writings. Allow whatever is on your mind to surface for each question.
3. Don't stress at all. If you only write a sentence, that's okay. If you want to write much more, that's okay too.

What you will find before the thirty days is complete, is that your answers evolve. By the end, you will have a much clearer understanding of who you are, where you are going, and why you are going there.

Is it worth your time to take a few minutes for a few days to come to see more of who you are and where you are headed? The return on investment on this exercise is literally beyond measure.

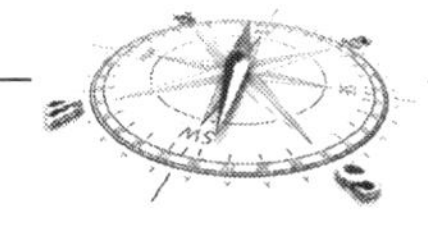

EXERCISE 9

# Personal Vision

To create your personal vision, carefully think about and answer each of the questions below. I recommend you take your time, perhaps over several days, to allow you to think deeply about each question. Do not worry about the length of your responses, as either short or long can be good. The important thing is to clarify and refine each.

**Question 1** – Who am I?

**Question 2** – What are my dreams?

**Question 3** – Who do I want to become?

**Question 4** – What are the top ten items on my bucket list?

— continued on next page —

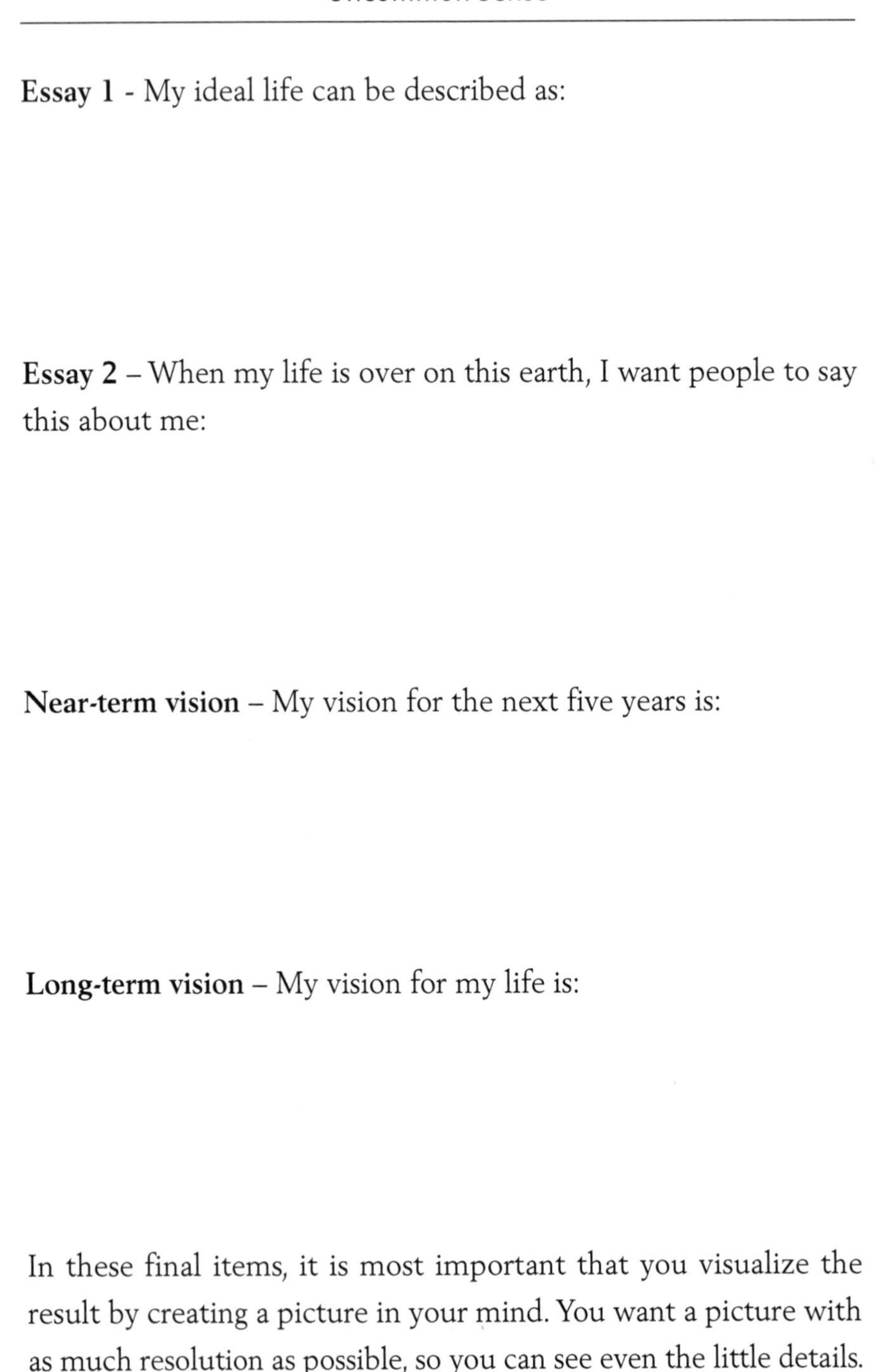

**Essay 1** - My ideal life can be described as:

**Essay 2** – When my life is over on this earth, I want people to say this about me:

**Near-term vision** – My vision for the next five years is:

**Long-term vision** – My vision for my life is:

In these final items, it is most important that you visualize the result by creating a picture in your mind. You want a picture with as much resolution as possible, so you can see even the little details.

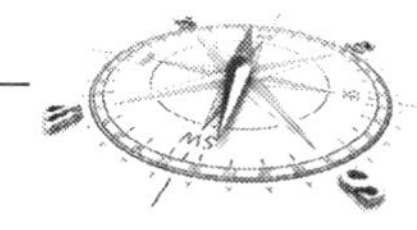

# Recommended Resources and Reading

Following are a number of books that have made a tremendous impact on my ability to navigate life. I highly recommend each of them and suggest using online videos sources such as YouTube, Vimeo, TED, and other such services to dig into the voluminous topics they cover.

You can find excellent videos and recordings on virtually anything you wish to know or learn about online.

| *Author* | *Book Title* |
| --- | --- |
| Allen, James | As a Man Thinketh |
| Arbinger Institute | Leadership and Self-Deception |
| Arbinger Institute | The Anatomy of Peace |
| Arbinger Institute | The Outward Mindset |
| Berger, Jennifer | Changing on the Job: Developing Leaders for a Complex World |
| Block, Peter | Stewardship |

| | |
|---|---|
| Boyatzis, Richard | Resonant Leadership |
| Buford, Bob | Half Time |
| Carnegie, Dale | How to Win Friends and Influence People |
| Cameron, Julia | The Artist's Way |
| Cashman, Kevin | The Pause Principle |
| Cashman, Kevin | Leadership from the Inside Out |
| Cashman Kevin | Awakening the Leader Within |
| Cole, Edwin | Courage |
| Cole, Edwin | Never Quit |
| Cole, Edwin | Treasure |
| Cole, Edwin | Maximized Manhood |
| Cooper, Robert K. | The Other 90% |
| Covey, Stephen | The 7 Habits of Highly Effective People |
| Dweck, Carol S. | Mindset |
| Drucker, Peter | The Effective Executive |
| Drucker, Peter | Managing Oneself |
| Duhigg, Charles | The Power of Habit |
| Emerald, David | The Power of TED |
| Fettke, Richard | Extreme Success |
| Fritz, Robert | The Path of Least Resistance |
| Gerber, Michael | The E-Myth |
| Gottman, John | The Seven Principles of Making Marriage Work |
| Goulston, Mark | Just Listen |
| Helmstetter, Shad | Who Are You and What Do You Really Want? |
| Kegan and Lahey | Immunity to Change |
| Goleman, Daniel | Emotional Intelligence |

| | |
|---|---|
| Lynn, Adele B. | The EQ Difference |
| Jennings and Stahl-Wert | The Serving Leader |
| Keller, Gary | The One Thing |
| Lencioni, Patrick | The Four Obsessions of an Extraordinary Executive |
| Lencioni, Patrick | Death by Meeting |
| Lencioni, Patrick | The Five Dysfunctions of a Team |
| May, Gerald G. | Addiction & Grace |
| McGee, Robert S. | The Search for Significance |
| Maxwell, John | The 21 Irrefutable Laws of Leadership |
| Maxwell, John | Thinking for a Change |
| Peck, M. Scott | The Road Less Traveled |
| Pink, Daniel H. | Drive |
| Rock, David | Your Brain at Work |
| Rohn, Jim | The Seasons of Life |
| Rohn, Jim | 7 Strategies for Wealth and Happiness |
| Scott, Steven K. | Simple Steps to Impossible Dreams |
| Seligman, Martin P. | Learned Optimism |
| Smalley, Gary | The DNA of Relationships |
| Tozer, A.W. | The Pursuit of God |
| Zander, R. and B. | The Art of Possibility |

Made in the USA
Middletown, DE
30 July 2019